MASTERING
Mindful Eating

MASTERING
Mindful Eating

Transform Your Relationship with Food
Plus 30 Recipes to Engage the Senses

MICHELLE BABB, MS, RD, CD

Photography by Hilary McMullen

SASQUATCH BOOKS
SEATTLE

To every person who was ever told their body was anything less than perfect, and for every gorgeous being who was ever put on a diet when they should have been having a pizza party with friends. This book is for you, along with my sincere belief that you will find a path of ease, joy, and contentment through mindful living.

Printed in China

SASQUATCH BOOKS with colophon is a registered trademark of Penguin Random House LLC

24 23 22 21 20   9 8 7 6 5 4 3 2 1

Editor: Jennifer Worick | Production editors: Bridget Sweet and Jill Saginario
Designer: Alicia Terry | Photography: Hilary McMullen | Food styling: Nathan Carrabba

Library of Congress Cataloging-in-Publication Data
Names: Babb, Michelle, author. | McMullen, Hilary, photographer.
Title: Mastering mindful eating : transform your relationship with food, plus 30
recipes to engage the senses / Michelle Babb, MS, RD, CD ; photography by Hilary McMullen.
Identifiers: LCCN 2020006194 (print) | LCCN 2020006195 (ebook) | ISBN
9781632172945 (paperback) | ISBN 9781632172952 (ebook)
Subjects: LCSH: Quick and easy cooking. | Mindfulness (Psychology) | LCGFT: Cookbooks.
Classification: LCC TX833.5 .B33 2020 (print) | LCC TX833.5 (ebook) | DDC 641.5/12--dc23
LC record available at https://lccn.loc.gov/2020006194
LC ebook record available at https://lccn.loc.gov/2020006195

ISBN: 978-1-63217-294-5

Sasquatch Books
1904 Third Avenue, Suite 710
Seattle, WA 98101
SasquatchBooks.com

Contents

Recipes to Engage Your Senses

What Is Mindful Eating?

PART I

diet

verb   di·et \ˈdī-ət\

*Restrict oneself to small amounts or special
kinds of food in order to lose weight.*

Source: *Oxford Dictionary of English*

Restriction. Deprivation. Shame. Guilt. Frustration. Disappointment. Failure.
These are all words that accurately describe the setup of our chronic dieting
culture. There is a multibillion-dollar industry built entirely on the premise
of keeping people forever fearful of gaining weight and desperate to find "the
best way" to lose it. It's called the dieting industry and it has made this business of eating *way too complicated.*

Eating your way to a sustainable weight and optimal health is simpler
than it seems. In fact, you were born to do it. We all have the innate sensibilities to tell us what to eat, when to eat, and *how* to eat, but we learn
how to override those cues at a very early age and then we spend a lifetime
neglecting our bodies and ignoring the signals that tell us everything we
ever needed to know. We're also manipulated by ingredients in processed
foods and fast food that are designed to cause cravings and fuel the desire
for *more.*

Have you ever heard that weight loss is a simple "calories in, calories
out" equation? That's how calorie counting became an obsession and the
grams of fat, carbs, and protein on the nutrition facts panel became the lit-
mus test for evaluating food. I call this *the science of eating*, where the focus
is squarely on calories and single nutrients in food. It ignores the synergistic
qualities of all the complex compounds in foods and completely discounts
the energetic properties of the foods we eat. And while there is a reality to
the effectiveness of caloric control, we're going about it the wrong way. For
most people, being accountable for every morsel of food they consume

(through tracking, logging, and paying penance for their food sins) is completely unsustainable. Not to mention that the nutritional quality of the food matters. We now have more information to add into the mix: we know that the foods we eat actually speak to our genes, greatly influencing gene expression, and our diet and lifestyle choices also impact the microbiome in the gut.

What if you could find your way back to that magical place where you trust your body enough to allow *it* to dictate what, when, and how you eat? Where you listen intently to how your body is communicating with you and you respond accordingly. This is when you give up that war against your body, abandon the idea of trying to beat it into submission, and instead create a lasting partnership with your body that's based on trust, respect, and love. I refer to this as *the art of eating*.

diet

noun di·et \ˈdī-ət\

Perpetual self-nourishment.

"Diet" doesn't have to be a dirty word. It can describe a nurturing way of feeding yourself. It's the ultimate act of self-care and it has to be done mindfully, with purpose and intention. People in our Western culture don't just accidentally eat well. Americans are confronted with over two hundred decisions about food and eating *every single day*. Living in the land of plenty actually makes the art of eating considerably more difficult. We're constantly distracted by flashy packaging, compelling advertising, and clever food marketing strategies. Couple that with a pattern of mindless eating and you've got the perfect formula for a nation of people who are chronically overfed and undernourished.

I teach classes and lead workshops on mindful eating. I ask my patients to unplug and treat this sacred act of self-nourishment as if it's an important event that deserves their undivided attention. When they practice this way of eating, amazing things happen. Not surprisingly, people eat less when they give themselves time to recognize satiety cues and they feel more satisfied after eating. Through slow, steady breathing and relaxation, the body shifts from fight-or-flight to rest-and-digest mode and the food moves through the digestive tract more easily and nutrients are readily absorbed.

This book is a compilation of the tools I've used with thousands of patients over the years, many of whom have successfully broken free from the dieting mentality and continue to enjoy a healthy, satisfying relationship with food. As you navigate your way through the book, take time to actually do the activities and reflect on your experiences. You may get stuck in some of the sections, and it may feel like it's taking you longer than expected to really "get it." Remember that you're trying to change some well-worn psychological pathways that you've been using for decades. You're trying to forge new pathways and you'll undoubtedly bump up against some resistance. That's part of the process, and it's totally normal. Give yourself some grace and practice patience as part of your self-care routine.

I even have patients who start to panic several weeks into the program despite getting great results. They wonder if they'll continue to see results if they don't have to suffer and feel deprived. That's when the deprogramming really begins. You have to prove to yourself that nourishing food can taste good, mindful eating is the best method for portion control, and you *deserve* to feel joyful and powerful in your body.

This program is not intended for those who want to drop twenty pounds in two weeks. It's a journey of self-exploration, reflection, and the creation of new thoughts, feelings, and behaviors. *Mastering Mindful Eating* helps you find your way home so that you can forever give up the struggle and create a lasting partnership with your amazing body. I hope you're excited to embark on this journey!

The Science of Eating versus the Art of Eating

A Sad, Sad History of Soul-Sucking Diets

A review of the last one hundred years of dieting is both comical and tragic. Comical because there have been so many outrageous recommendations through the ages (vibrating massage belts, bile beans, fat-melting soaps, or tapeworm ingestion, anyone?) and tragic because the weight-loss industry is still at it, more aggressively than ever. It still promotes punishing programs with fleeting results and desperate dieters are seeing their pocketbooks get thinner while their waistlines continue to expand. Perhaps the recommendations may be somewhat more civilized (debatable), but marketers still prey on body insecurities and media-fueled feelings of inadequacy.

Dieting is not a new idea. The word "diet" originated from the Greek word *diaita*, which actually referred to a much broader concept than just controlling food intake. It was a more holistic perspective that acknowledged other lifestyle factors as equal contributors to overall health and wellness. The ancient Greek philosophy that a healthy mind and body makes for a healthy society seems like a vast improvement over the predominant thin-at-any-cost mentality of today.

Award-winning historian Louise Foxcroft provides a revealing look at the absolute absurdity of our dieting culture in her brilliant book *Calories & Corsets*. There are many jaw-dropping descriptions of diets in her book, but one overarching concept that really caught my attention was that historically the ideal body was thought to be male and the female form was actually regarded as "pathological." It's no wonder that finding a way to the perfect body has been more difficult for women, with their problematic curves and concealed muscles. The struggle is real! Or so we've been programmed to believe.

This is not to say that men don't struggle with their weight, and in fact many of the first diets on record were developed by men. Take for instance Lord Byron, a famous poet from the 1820s who struggled mightily to keep his body sexy and trim. His strategy? The vinegar and water diet, which involved drinking that combo several times a day to flush out the fat. It was reported that some of his adoring fans (mostly women) died from drinking pints of vinegar. This hunky poet was also known for binge eating, then starving himself while wearing several layers of clothing to sweat off the pounds. Many call Lord Byron the first celebrity dieter.

And then there was William Banting, whose name became synonymous with dieting. He was an early adopter of the low-carb diet way back in the 1860s. Perhaps you thought low-carb eating was introduced with the Paleo concept, Whole30, or the ketogenic diet? Nope! This diet has been failing us for more than 150 years. We just keep repackaging it and calling it something new. Banting was an Englishman who lost fifty pounds in a year by eating almost nothing more than meat three times a day. I would rename Banting's plan the "Prime Yourself for Colon Cancer Diet."

Maybe focusing attention on the mechanics of eating would be a better way to go, thought Horace Fletcher, an overweight art dealer who needed to shed some pounds to qualify for life insurance around the turn of the century. Fletcher lost forty pounds by chewing each mouthful of food a minimum of thirty-two times (once for each tooth in your mouth). His recommendations were to liquefy the food in your mouth, then swallow the liquid but spit out the remaining fiber. Think of all the money he saved on toilet paper because he reportedly pooped only twice a week. He also suggested eating only when extremely hungry and preferably not when angry or sad. While parts of this are akin to mindful eating, don't get too excited.

Horace Fletcher became increasingly obsessed with refining his diet and eventually ate so little fiber that constipation became debilitating and his nutrient intake was so low that he couldn't fight off simple infections and died of pneumonia at age sixty-nine. Fletcherism had a fairly long run from 1905 to the mid-1930s. That's *a lot* of chewing! Not to mention a whole new market for laxatives.

Calorie counting made its first appearance in a book published in 1918 by Dr. Lulu Hunt Peters titled *Dieting and Health: With Key to the Calories*. Dr. Peters had some personal experience with the battle of bulge, once weighing 220 pounds herself. She advocated a 1,200-calorie diet for women, eaten in 100-calorie units throughout the day. Analyzing and recording calories was not an easy task at the time, but the calories-in, calories-out formula is still the predominant driver for weight-loss plans. Today, plenty of apps make it easier than ever to stop trusting your body and start scanning, entering, and analyzing every morsel of food that goes into your body. Oh goody! More quality time with our cell phones.

Clever magazine and print ads helped reinforce the business of weight loss, targeting mostly women with various products that were said to be the panacea for a slender figure. Desperate times call for desperate measures and truth in advertising wasn't really a thing yet, so pretty much any claim could be made. My personal favorite? Cigarette ads that encouraged taking up smoking as a way to manage sweet cravings. Because if you wanna develop emphysema or lung cancer, you wanna look good while you're doing it.

When cigarettes became an unacceptable form of weight control (or at least one you couldn't advertise because of the cancer problem), there were plenty of other dangerous options that were becoming quite popular, mostly in the form of diet pills—amphetamines (speed), dinitrophenol, ephedra, phenylpropanolamine, and deadly combinations of all of the above. You might remember the Fen-Phen debacle, which was a diet drug made from fenfluramine and phentermine that was approved for obesity treatment after one small study and was later shown to cause heart-valve damage. Fen-Phen was pulled from the market and more than $4.8 billion was paid out in settlements. Imagine my surprise when a patient came in a few months ago and sheepishly told me that her doctor had prescribed the new and improved Fen-Phen, which is just phentermine combined with an antiseizure med called topiramate. Keep in mind this patient was not obese but wanted to accelerate her thirty-pound weight-loss goal. Common side effects of this drug include constipation, insomnia, inflammation of the throat and nasal passages, mood disorder, sleep disorder, dizziness, nausea, and fatigue, to name a few.

And speaking of life-altering side effects of diet drugs, how about the miracle drug Alli (orlistat) that helps block fat absorption so most of it will just come right out in your poo. We know we've reached a whole new level of desperation when we're willing to overlook side effects like fatty/oily stools, oily spotting in your undergarments, intestinal gas with discharge (also charmingly known as sharting), and bowel urgency. I'm pretty sure this was the drug my mom was prescribed by a diet doctor, who added this sage advice: "Just take one. If you take two, you'll poop your pants."

Diet drugs are not going away anytime soon. I mean, Big Pharma clearly would not pass up the opportunity to be part of the multibillion-dollar dieting machine. In fact, according to GlobalData, a leading data and analytics company, six new drugs targeting obesity are anticipated to be released in the United States by 2026. Of course, it wouldn't make sense to completely solve the problem of overweight and obesity because that might cut into profits from all the drugs needed to treat what are viewed as obesity-related diseases like type 2 diabetes and heart disease.

The '60s, '70s, and '80s ushered in another wave of food- or nutrient-specific diets like acid-alkaline diets, food combining, the Hollywood Grapefruit Diet, the Scarsdale Diet, and let's not forget the Master Cleanse, which involves drinking nothing but water with lemon juice, maple syrup, and a dash of cayenne pepper six to twelve times per day. I *still* make desperate pleas for people not to try this diet when the New Year rolls around.

In 1972, American cardiologist Dr. Robert Atkins published *Dr. Atkins' Diet Revolution*, which revitalized concepts from the early 1800s that cutting out carbs and eating mostly meat and fat would be a marvelous idea. The diet was controversial among health and medical experts, but Americans loved it because, let's face it, people like bacon a lot more than they like fruit. There was no counting calories; instead, just give up starchy veggies, grains, beans, and fruit, and eat all the meat and dairy you need to feel full (salads were encouraged, to be fair). Atkins died at the age of seventy-two from a head injury after slipping on the ice, but the medical examiner's report revealed that he had a history of heart attack, congestive heart failure, and hypertension. Just sayin'—you can draw your own conclusions. Atkins came from the back from the dead, or at least some iteration of his corporation did, and launched *Dr. Atkins' New Diet Revolution* in 1992.

Let's pause for a moment to acknowledge that the extreme diet strategies of the ages have been created mostly by men and targeted primarily at women. So when do the women start taking the reins? In the early '60s Jean Nidetch, a gregarious housewife from Queens, was fed up with a lifetime of emotional eating, roller-coaster dieting, and an insatiable cookie addiction. She invited six overweight friends to meet in her living room, where they vowed to support one another in efforts to the lose weight once and for all. Nidetch shed seventy-two pounds, which she successfully kept off for the rest of her life. She founded Weight Watchers in 1963. This was one of first programs to acknowledge that food addiction and overeating is an emotional problem, which must be addressed through group support, education, and accountability. Weight Watchers was based on a system where points were assigned to foods and participants were allotted a certain number of points per day. Millions of dieters have joined the Weight Watchers program through the years and it's still going strong today. It's commonly the top-ranked diet program. It has softened its position on the point system and incorporated mindful eating into its program.

Jenny Craig opened her weight-loss centers, first in Australia in 1983, then in the United States in 1985. Craig had difficulty losing weight after the birth of her first child and was keen on providing the human touch through weight-loss counseling and ease and convenience through prepackaged foods. *U.S. News & World Report* ranks Jenny Craig as the second most-effective commercial weight-loss program after Weight Watchers.

The fitness craze of the '80s and early '90s brought more women onto the scene. Jane Fonda became every woman's workout buddy. We were getting physical with Olivia Newton-John, Jazzercising with friends, and ordering Suzanne Somers's ThighMaster. While we were busy obsessing with burning away the fat on our bodies, diet trends turned toward low-fat diets. This is what I like to call "the SnackWell's era." If you were around for this low-fat, fat-free period, you undoubtedly discovered that bright-green box of cookies, which were made from white flour and five different types of sugar. But hey, they were fat-free! And, of course, that meant you could eat as many as you wanted.

I wish this brought me to an end of the bad fad diet story, but alas, the hits just keep on coming. The last couple of decades have brought us the Zone Diet, South Beach Diet (one of the saner diet plans, by the way), Medifast, Dukan Diet, Ornish Diet (yay for more veggies!), Volumetrics, Fit for Life, DASH, Paleo, keto, and the list goes on. In case you're thinking, "at least modern diets don't rely on crazy tactics like ingesting tapeworms," just wait. There are plenty of asinine commercial diets that generations to come will be scoffing at in disbelief. These include the Werewolf Diet (where you fast according to the moon cycles), the Cotton Ball Diet (revived from the 1950s, it involves ingesting cotton balls dipped in liquid to feel full), and the KE diet (for those who don't have the discipline to follow the ketogenic diet, you can arrange to have a nasogastric tube placed so there's no way of cheating on this eight-hundred-calorie per day, no-carb diet).

In the face of all these diets, Americans are getting fatter and sicker, and childhood obesity rates are still on the rise. Diets have a 95 to 97 percent failure rate, yet we keep thinking we'll get different results. That's the definition of insanity and it's creating a crisis of the mind, body, and spirit. There's only one response to all of this . . . **F*ck dieting!**

The Science of Eating

When I made the decision to go back to school in my midthirties to earn a master of science in nutrition and become a registered dietitian, I consulted with Dr. Buck Levin, a friend and former colleague who is a registered dietitian and a professor at Bastyr University. I was weighing my options and wondering if I should just choose the path that would be least disruptive to my work life. I was an executive at a public relations firm and thinking I might still be able to work and take classes online or at night. I had dreams of going to Bastyr, an accredited university in Kenmore, Washington, that teaches holistic medicine and personalized nutrition, but it was a full-time program with no evening classes. When I told Buck I was looking at online programs or an evening program at a local university instead, he said, "You already know too much to be happy with that decision. You won't be satisfied with the classic single-nutrient approach to food and nutrition, where you learn how to analyze the nutrition facts panel and memorize the RDAs [recommended daily allowances for nutrients]."

That conversation with Buck sealed the deal for me. Not to mention that my dear friend and mentor, Barb Schiltz, who had completed the program at Bastyr herself, had been encouraging me to apply for years. I took the plunge and was so grateful I did. Bastyr provided a more integrative view of nutrition. Classes like Whole Foods Nutrition and Cooking with Whole Foods were mandatory. Cooking classes were actually part of the program! Don't get me wrong, this is an evidence-based program that's accredited by the Academy of Nutrition and Dietetics, so I didn't escape biochemistry, biostatistics, or macro- and micronutrients. But I was at home at Bastyr because it blended the science and art of food and nutrition.

The science of eating has historically been focused on calorie consumption and single nutrients, which tends to neglect the complexity and synergistic nature of food and the many physiological variabilities that alter our biological response to eating. Not to mention that our food supply has become so incredibly processed that single-nutrient studies don't even begin to cover all the ingredients we're ingesting daily. The Food and Drug Administration (FDA) maintains a list of more than three thousand ingredients in its database called "Substances Added to Food in the United States." While these ingredients have been granted GRAS status (generally recognized as safe), that really just means we aren't likely to drop dead on the spot from eating them. Many ingredients have had their GRAS status revoked and been banned from use by food manufacturers only after links to cancer or other disabling diseases become apparent in the research after years of consumption.

JUST THE FACTS, MA'AM

What we're left with is a nutrition facts panel that was mandated in 1990 and still contains very little meaningful information. Recent "improvements" include making the calorie count larger and bolder, listing added sugars, and standardizing portion sizes. None of this solves the biggest problem with the nutrition facts panel, which is that it oversimplifies the complexity of food and inevitably leads to overvaluing the numbers and undervaluing the actual ingredients in the food.

There's so much more to the story than what's highlighted on the nutrition facts panel and if you give too much credence to what fits inside that box, you are likely to overlook the many factors that paint *your* unique picture of health and wellness. You are an original work of art that's forever in the making. While you can use what science provides to help explain and understand how your body functions and what type of fuel it needs, it's important to embrace your biochemical uniqueness and rely on the wisdom that lies within.

PROBLEMS WITH THE NUTRITION FACTS PANEL

CONFUSING CARB COUNT

Carbs have become the new fat, and carb-phobic consumers discount fiber and confuse natural forms of sugar like the lactose in dairy products or the fructose in fruit with added sugars.

ONE SIZE FITS ALL

All of the percentage daily values are based on a 2,000-calorie diet, so the percent daily value will be off for those with different energy needs or specific nutrient needs, which is most of us.

Nutrition Facts

about 6 servings per container

Serving size	1 cup (140g)

Amount per serving

Calories	170

	% Daily Value*
Total Fat 8g	10%
Saturated Fat 3g	15%
Trans Fat 0g	
Cholesterol 0mg	0%
Sodium 5mg	0%
Total Carbohydrate 22g	8%
Dietary Fiber 2g	7%
Total Sugars 16g	
Includes 8g Added Sugars	16%
Protein 2g	
Vitamin D 0mcg	0%
Calcium 20mg	2%
Iron 1mg	6%
Potassium 240mg	6%

*The % Daily Value (DV) tells you how much a nutrient in a serving of food contributes to a daily diet. 2,000 calories a day is used for general nutrition advice.

PORTION DISTORTION

Despite standardization of serving sizes, most consumers still overlook how many servings are in one container. Notice there are 6 servings in this package.

CALORIE OBSESSION

The larger, bolder calorie count is just a reminder that we're still perpetuating a calorie-obsessed culture and making this seem like the most important piece of nutrition information on the package.

MICROSCOPIC INGREDIENT LIST

As the nutrition facts panel becomes bigger and bolder, there's even less room on the packaging for the most important piece of information . . . the list of ingredients! As a general rule of thumb, if you need a magnifying glass and a translator to help you figure out what the hell is in your food, put it back on the shelf and head straight to the produce section.

CALORIES IN, CALORIES OUT, BLAH, BLAH, BLAH

Math is hard. If you don't like the idea of tallying up your daily calories from the nutrition facts panels (even though it's now in *big, bold* font), well . . . there's an app for that. In fact, there are numerous apps that will count up your daily calories and nutrients, some that even allow you to scan food product bar codes to get the most accurate nutritional assessment of the processed foods you're eating. I'm willing to concede that people who record their food intake and track their calories tend to eat less when they're in the tracking mode. However, recording every morsel of food you put in your mouth becomes a part-time job and not many people have the time or energy to commit to a lifetime of tracking.

Obsessive tracking can also be stress producing and can alter your relationship with food in an unfavorable way. A study involving women assigned to one of four groups (monitoring plus restricting, monitoring only, restricting only, and control) concluded that both restricting and monitoring food intake caused stress, with monitoring being categorized as psychological stress. When I ask my patients to take a break from daily food tracking, the most common response I get is one of relief. Even those who are skeptical and reluctant at first often come back and report feeling less obsessed with food and happy to get relief from the constant feedback the tracking apps provide.

Much like the earlier point-counting system used by Weight Watchers, food-tracking apps with calorie counting encourages you to reduce food to mere numbers, and you will inevitably alter decisions about foods based solely on how many calories that food will add to your bottom line. One might overlook all the magical, synergistic properties of an avocado, for example, simply because it contributes over two hundred calories and around twenty grams of fat. Or people will bank their points in order to gorge on a "cheat meal," or maybe an alcohol binge.

Tracking also serves as a constant reminder that you can't be trusted to tune into your own body wisdom. This, of course, is the wisdom you were born with and it's always there, waiting to guide you and hoping that you will take the time to listen and respond accordingly. One of the many great things about mindfulness as an alternative to tracking is that it doesn't require more time. It just means that you're paying attention to what you're doing and how you're feeling in the moments that you are already living. Sure, if you're a chronic multitasker it takes some getting used to, but you don't have to set aside minutes or hours of your day to find time for mindfulness. You can simply integrate it into everything you're already doing.

The Art of Eating

Ironically, we've spent so much time trying to figure out what to eat and what to avoid that we've completely lost sight of the importance of *how* we eat. And quite frankly, American eating habits are atrocious. I know that mindful eating is a novel concept because I'm told time and again by my patients that this is the first conversation they've ever had about the manner in which they eat. There's a yes-or-no question on my patient intake form that asks, "Are you typically multitasking while eating (e.g., working on the computer, checking cell phone, watching TV)?" At least 95 percent reply yes. The question is followed by, "What is your pace of eating on a scale from 1 to 5 with 1 being extremely slow?" The vast majority of multitaskers rank their pace as a 4 or 5.

I'm not sure whether to blame it on our dieting culture, our technology obsession, or societal pressure to constantly be multitasking in every area of our lives, but it's not leading us anywhere good. What I know to be true is that we are now a culture of very anxious eaters, with a host of digestive problems and an inability to self-regulate. I also know that intentional, mindful eating provides a solution to these problems.

A review of intuitive eating programs looked at twenty different interventions and overall there were improvements in eating habits, lifestyle, and body image. Participants also experienced improved psychological health with less depression and anxiety, higher self-esteem, and improved quality of life. The best part is that several of these improvements held through follow-up periods as long as two years and completion rates were as high as 92 percent, which is unheard of in restrictive dieting studies.

CAROLINE'S STORY

Caroline came to me just as she was getting ready to turn fifty. She had Hashimoto's thyroiditis and had a hysterectomy a year prior due to ovarian cancer. Her weight was not budging since the hysterectomy, despite religiously tracking her macros and engaging in some physical activity. She was fatigued and discouraged.

Caroline would go long periods without eating and then find herself binging in the evening. She admitted to being a fast eater in general and was often multitasking while eating. The first order of business was to give her a break from tracking, balance her food plan, and close the gaps so she wasn't starving at the end of the day. The other goal was to slow her pace of eating.

When Caroline returned she was visibly more energetic and was delighted by how much of a difference it made to incorporate an afternoon snack and to slow down and pay attention to how she was eating. Cravings had dissipated and weight was slowly coming off. "I'm not starving anymore *and* I'm losing weight. Who knew?!" she exclaimed.

Four months later, after a few more sessions, Caroline was sharing her success with all her friends. "It's so simple. I just know this is the way to eat," she told me. Her energy continued to improve, her immune system was stronger, and she came home to her body.

HEALTH BENEFITS OF SLOWING DOWN AND SAVORING

What if you were to treat eating like a sacred ritual? Instead of grabbing whatever is closest and most convenient, what if you actually planned and prepared wholesome food that you feel really good about eating? And what if you sat down and focused on the business of eating without distraction or worry? Just you and the food. How do you think your body would respond? You might be surprised at how different it feels to engage with your food in a thoughtful and respectful way. Here are the ways in which your body, mind, and spirit benefit from this way of eating:

· When you slow down and sit with your food for a minute before eating it, you might actually start to salivate, which is the first step in digestion so you're already giving your GI system a head start.

· If you take a deep breath before you start eating and allow your body to relax, you've called up your parasympathetic nervous system, which puts you in the rest-and-digest state.

· No distractions or external stressors help you stay in the parasympathetic state while you eat, which gives your body a well-deserved break from the general craziness of the day and allows your adrenals to take a rest.

· When you take a moment to smell your food, it enhances the taste and you get more pleasure out of eating.

· Putting your fork down between bites and really chewing your food also aids in digestion and gives you time to recognize you're satisfied before you're stuffed.

· Completing your eating ritual before you move on to other tasks allows your body to feel nourished and your mind to feel clearer and more focused.

· Treating mealtime like a mini-meditation is good for your soul and is much less likely to leave you wanting and craving than eating as if you're in a fire drill.

Physiological Influencers

We are adaptive creatures by nature, which generally serves us well and allows us to enjoy a very long life span. The downside of adaptation is that we learn to live with chronic health problems that we chalk up to aging or just stop noticing altogether. Sometimes they're small things, like an itchy scalp or dry eyes, other times they're more serious issues like abdominal pain, irritable bowel syndrome (IBS), chronic insomnia or sleep apnea, weakness and fatigue, chronic inflammation, or neurodegenerative disorders. When your body is working hard to deal with a more chronic problem, it's too distracted to be bothered with good metabolism, optimal digestion, and clear thinking. It's like having the alarm bells go off in your body 24/7. Finding the root cause of these chronic conditions and dealing with them (ideally without pharmaceutical intervention) turns the alarm bells off and restores your body to its homeodynamic state, where metabolism, digestion, and focus/attention can become priorities again.

MAKE LIKE A ZEBRA AND LET GO OF THE STRESS

Stress in and of itself is not a bad thing. We need to activate the stress response to be able to function in our environment. It's when stress becomes chronic that it presents a problem. One of the most illuminating descriptions of acute versus chronic stress can be seen in Robert Sapolsky's book *Why Zebras Don't Get Ulcers*. The premise is that zebras know how to do stress. On a typical day, you would find said zebra grazing out in the Serengeti without a care in the world when suddenly a lion appears and starts to chase after the zebra. The zebra has a major cortisol release, adrenaline is pumping, and the fight-or-flight reaction kicks into full gear so the zebra can run for her life. Once the zebra escapes the lion, she goes back to grazing in the sun with no lingering worry of the lion she just

FIGHT OR FLIGHT	REST AND DIGEST
(FAST & FURIOUS EATING)	(RELAXED & MINDFUL EATING)

Uh-oh! Cotton mouth. Less saliva production means fewer enzymes to start breaking down the food.	Saliva is flowing! And that's great news because you've already started the process of digestion before you even swallow. Those amylase enzymes in your saliva break down starches.
Your liver converts glycogen into glucose and releases it into the bloodstream for fast fuel.	Your lovely liver stimulates bile release from your gallbladder and that's gonna help you break down fat.
↑ BLOOD GLUCOSE	DIGESTIVE ENZYMES ↑
The pancreas goes on strike and halts production of digestive enzymes and refrains from releasing insulin.	Stomach juices increase and your pancreas happily produces and releases digestive enzymes so your food can be broken down into nutrients that get absorbed in your small intestine.
↓ NUTRIENT ABSORPTION	NUTRIENT ABSORPTION ↑
Stalled-out peristalsis makes it harder for food to move through the digestive tract and can affect elimination.	Peristalsis induces wavelike muscle contractions that keep moving the food through the digestive tract while waste makes its way to the colon for healthy elimination. Smooth move!
↑ BLOATING & IRREGULAR BM	EFFICIENT ELIMINATION

encountered nor any concerns about predators that she'll encounter in the future. Her nervous system immediately goes back into parasympathetic mode so that she can rest and digest the food she's grazing on. Now *that* is a productive stress response.

How can we humans be more like zebras? All roads lead back to mindfulness. Jon Kabat-Zinn's approach to mindfulness-based stress reduction may just be the solution. Much like the zebra, if you are just focused on what is happening in the present moment there is no room for overreacting to stressors from the past or stressors in the future.

A research review confirmed that perceived stressful experiences and psychosocial strain (e.g., arguments with family members, disputes in the workplace, financial concerns, etc.) are positively correlated with higher body mass index (BMI) and waist circumference and stress-related eating was identified as one clear contributor.

VIVA LAS VAGUS!

Stimulating the vagus nerve, which runs from your brain stem to the base of your abdomen, is a signal to your body to switch from fight or flight to rest and digest. A few fun ways to tickle your vagus nerve include:

- Yoga
- Meditation
- Acupuncture
- Forest bathing (yep, that's walking in the woods)
- Biofeedback (using tools to monitor things like heart rate variability or body temperature while you practice relaxation techniques)

I have to admit to having a holy-crap moment when I was reading a study that examined how stress shuts down some of the functions in the prefrontal cortex of the brain. That's the most evolved region of the brain and it plays an important role in intelligent regulation of thoughts, actions, and emotions. This study goes on to say that "even quite mild acute uncontrollable stress can cause a rapid and dramatic loss of prefrontal cognitive abilities." Among those abilities is the flexible regulation of behaviors and inhibition of inappropriate actions. This explains why those who engage in stress eating feel a loss of control over their actions and often report binging or overeating while on autopilot.

The bottom line is that our stress response can be adaptive and helpful if our body can turn it on when it's needed and off when it's not. When resilience to stress is low, the response to even minor stressors can be disproportionate and prolonged. That's when your body will start to communicate by showing you the symptoms of stress overload: fatigue, brain fog, emotional variability, digestive distress, and an increase in abdominal fat. If you're listening carefully, you'll hear your body asking you for a reprieve from chronic stress. The simple act of taking a deep belly breath and/or thinking about something for which you are grateful can help change your physiology and allow your body to take a rest from stress.

YOU ARE GETTING VERRRRRY SLEEEEPY

Sleep is another commodity that seems increasingly hard to come by. An estimated 35 percent of Americans report getting fewer than seven hours of sleep per night. This is a problem, since research shows that our bodies and brains work best when we get between seven and nine hours of sleep. Personally, I never understood what a physiological hardship it is to be chronically underslept until I hit perimenopause and lost my ability to sleep through the night. Not only did I feel anxious and fatigued, but it impacted my blood pressure and blood glucose. I could suddenly relate to my patients who were desperately seeking a good night's sleep.

Some of the physiological consequences associated with lack of sleep include insulin resistance, weight gain and obesity, high triglycerides, high blood pressure, higher risk of cardiovascular disease, and type 2 diabetes. There's also a bidirectional relationship between sleep and depression/anxiety and fibromyalgia. A secondary consequence is that persistent fatigue can make it challenging to stay motivated to make meaningful lifestyle changes. Many of my patients complain that they simply don't have the energy to be eating and exercising the way they want to be.

Sleep apnea (defined as involuntary cessation of breathing during sleep) is also a serious problem. According to the American Sleep Apnea Association (ASAA), an estimated twenty-two million Americans suffer from sleep apnea, with 80 percent of the cases of moderate and severe obstructive sleep apnea undiagnosed. The ASAA also notes that "too little good sleep appears to be as much a factor in obesity as too much food and too little exercise."

DO THESE MICROBES MAKE MY BUTT LOOK BIG?

Perhaps one of the biggest variables related to a person's ability to regulate weight is the state of his/her microbiome—the bacterial environment in the gut. Researchers have looked at the microbial makeup of the gut and found strong associations between obesity and limited diversity of microbes and/or an overabundance of a group of bacteria called Firmicutes. It appears that Firmicutes can actually extract more calories from food, so if that's the dominant form of bacteria in your gut you may actually be absorbing more calories than a person with a different microbial makeup. Pretty wild, right? Not only do Firmicutes play a role in regulating calorie absorption, but these little troops of microbes also influence how fat gets distributed in our bodies, how sensitive our cells are to the insulin signal, and our ability to produce hunger and satiety hormones.

Knowing this makes many fad diets even worse than we thought. Diets that severely limit complex carbohydrates (like beans, fruits, starchy veggies, and whole grains) and favor high fat or high protein lead to a messed-up microbiome that is ultimately working against you. The single most impactful dietary change to help restore your microbiome to good working order is to *eat more high-fiber, plant-based foods*. Forget what you've been told about fruit or yams or beets having "too much sugar." These are some of the best high-fiber foods *and* contain a plethora of disease-protecting phytonutrients *and* provide the fuel that the beneficial microbes need to thrive.

Probiotics have gotten a lot of attention, and with good reason. Cultured dairy, nut, and soy products as well as fermented foods are great for the gut. Many of my patients have started making their own ferments, which I wholeheartedly endorse. I do, however, provide some cautionary warnings about overdoing it with drinkable ferments like kombucha (fermented black tea). Too many of my patients started making their own kombucha and drinking it by the gallons. Digestion seemed to improve initially, then digestive function starts to get more variable with lots of bloating and irregular bowel movements. So just don't fall into the trap of "if a little is good, a lot is better!" That's not always the case.

We still have a lot to learn about how to cultivate a more symbiotic relationship with all the microbes we have on board, but we do know that changes in diet have an immediate effect on the microbial status in the gut. And in fact, changes can be seen after just one meal. As you're learning how to make more intentional food choices, part of your internal dialogue might be acknowledging that you're caring for your precious microbes and creating an environment where they can thrive.

LEAKY GUT, ROGUE BACTERIA, AND OTHER TUMMY TROUBLES

Is leaky gut a real thing? I get asked this a lot from patients who seem to be getting increasingly sensitive to the foods they eat and have a host of GI issues ranging from bloating and abdominal pain to diarrhea, constipation, nausea, and sometimes even vomiting. Many have been suffering for years and have looked to conventional medicine for solutions. They often come up empty. They've been poked, prodded, and scoped only to find there are no overt structural issues, so they walk away with a diagnosis of irritable bowel syndrome (IBS). If food or nutrition is mentioned at all, it's usually just to say something obvious like, "You can try avoiding the foods that seem to make you sick."

Well, I'm here to tell you that leaky gut (or intestinal permeability, if you want the more acceptable fancy term) is a real thing and IBS is a consequence of other problems. Sometimes if a food allergy or intolerance has gone unchecked for years, it creates an ongoing state of inflammation. Those inflammatory messengers in your gut start to loosen up the tight junctions in your intestinal tract and ta-da, you've got leaky gut. Now the food proteins that are supposed be traveling through the intestinal tract leak out and your body recognizes them as foreign invaders. Whenever I see a food allergy blood test that comes back showing sensitivities to over half the foods on the list, I'm suspicious of leaky gut.

Another common condition I've been seeing a lot in my practice over the last few years is small intestinal bacterial overgrowth (SIBO). Simply put, this is a condition where bacteria is congregating in the no-party zone of your small intestine, instead of staying where they belong in your lower intestine and colon. This produces severe bloating and discomfort after eating and is often accompanied by IBS-type symptoms. People with SIBO have a lot of difficulty eating beans, onions, garlic, and cruciferous vegetables. There's a breath test to determine whether you have SIBO and it's best to work with a practitioner who has a specific protocol to treat it.

Here's where my diet disclaimer comes in. I believe everything starts and ends in the gut, so treating GI issues is the first order of business. This often means that some sort of a therapeutic diet will be warranted. Sometimes we can handle it with a classic elimination diet. I once had a patient who was vomiting every single morning (and she definitely wasn't pregnant).

After a three-week elimination diet followed by food reintroductions, she discovered she had a severe sensitivity to eggs. She took them out of her diet and didn't vomit again. In the case of SIBO, patients may need to follow a low FODMAP (fermentable oligo-, di-, monosaccharides and polyols) or specific carbohydrate diet for a period while they're being treated. As I explain to my patients, these therapeutic diets should be considered a short-term solution to aid in healing, but the goal is to be able to expand the diet again once the gut is back to good working order.

I will say that nearly every patient who is struggling with digestive issues benefits greatly from mindful eating. These are patients who need to do everything in their power to optimize digestion, so slowing down, relaxing, and being in the rest-and-digest state while eating is critically important. This is the conversation I have with anyone who is doing a therapeutic diet under my watch. We also work on focusing on the healing foods they can eat, versus lamenting over the list of foods to temporarily avoid. I help patients safely transition from these therapeutic diets to a more expansive diet, encouraging them to tune into their bodies and pay attention to foods that help them feel strong and healthy in addition to noticing foods that are not serving them well.

HOLY HORMONES, WHAT'S HAPPENING TO ME?

Hormone levels change throughout our life cycle, but can also be influenced by, you guessed it, all the lifestyle factors in the spheres of wellness (nutrition, activity and movement, stress, sleep, and relationships/community). The vast majority of women I work with in my practice are between the ages of forty and sixty and are feeling like their bodies are becoming less predictable in perimenopause and menopause. Men also experience a shift in hormones later in life called andropause, which equates to less dehydroepiandrosterone (DHEA) and testosterone, usually as they approach their forties and fifties.

One large research review looked at various lifestyle factors, including meal composition and meal frequency, exercise, sleep, and psychological stress, and assessed how they influenced hormone levels. They concluded that the best overall recommendations for favorable hormonal balance are eating smaller, more frequent meals with moderate protein and lower fat, getting eight hours of sleep each night, exercising regularly but not with too much intensity, and controlling psychological stress. So in other words, very sensible recommendations that *have* withstood the test of time.

I like to remind my patients that they don't have to feel like they're entirely at the mercy of their hormones. In fact, that's where mindful eating steals third base and slides right into home. Slowing down the pace of eating and treating mealtime like a meditation reduces cortisol levels, provides a feeling of relaxation and well-being, reduces cravings for sugar (which is a big contributor to hormonal dysregulation), and helps with better insulin signaling and more reliable hunger and satiety cues.

HORMONES 101

Here's a quick overview of some of the key players when it comes to metabolism and weight variability:

- **Ghrelin:** stimulates appetite, influences sleep, controls gastric motility
- **Leptin:** produced and secreted by fat cells; responsible for satiety signals
- **Cortisol:** adrenal steroid that regulates response to stress; chronically high levels of circulating cortisol are associated with an increase in abdominal fat
- **Insulin:** secreted by the pancreas and utilized by the cells to regulate glucose; overproduction can result in insulin resistance, which leads to weight gain and metabolic dysfunction

- **Estrogen:** plays a role in insulin metabolism, energy expenditure, and prevention of inflammation and fat accumulation

- **Progesterone:** plays an important role in protein, fat, and carbohydrate metabolism; also impacts mood and sleep

- **Testosterone:** sex hormone found in men and women; important for muscle development and bone health

- **TSH:** thyroid stimulating hormone; regulated by a feedback loop in the thyroid gland; important for regulating metabolism

FOODS FOR HEALTHY HORMONE BALANCE

- Cruciferous vegetables
- Cabbage, broccoli, brussels sprouts, cauliflower, bok choy
- Leafy greens
- Spinach, kale, Swiss chard, collard greens, beet greens
- Soy (minimally processed)
- Edamame, tofu, tempeh, miso
- Berries, melon, and citrus
- Raw nuts and seeds
- Ground flaxseed
- Beans
- Whole grains
- Wild-caught fish
- Seaweed (great for sluggish thyroid!)
- Nori, dulse, arame, wakame, hijiki, and kombu

Blending Art and Science for Optimal Care

Many of my patients have benefited greatly from creating their own wellness support team that includes functional medicine practitioners and integrative health providers of various disciplines, such as nutrition, naturopathic medicine, acupuncture, counseling, physical therapy or structural integration, and energy healing. They may not work with all the practitioners on their care team all the time, but they can see who they need, when they need them, and the care can be collaborative when the support team shares ideas and strategies to help support the patient.

An integrative care team understands that there are various physiological, psychosocial, spiritual, and environmental contributors to health. I've designed my own model for trying to learn more about my patients and help them prioritize the areas that are needing attention. You'll learn how to use the spheres of wellness for your own self-assessment later in the book.

SPHERES OF WELLNESS

NUTRITION
Access to quality food
Nutritional deficiencies
Food allergies/intolerances
Eating behaviors
Genetic and epigenetic factors

**RELATIONSHIPS /
COMMUNITY**
Feeling supported
Having love in your life
Feeling needed
Having purpose
Feeling connected

SOURCE
(the essence of your being;
your highest self or your
belief in a higher power)

**ACTIVITY AND
MOVEMENT**
Ability and desire
Depression and fatigue
Pain and discomfort
Access to nature

SLEEP
Sleep hygiene
Medications
Circadian rhythm
Hormonal disruptions
Family/pets
disrupting sleep

STRESS
Financial security
Work or family stress
Depression/anxiety
Health issues
Limited coping
strategies

You are the subject of the grand experiment of your life. You are biochemically unique.

Stop the Struggle

You Are Not Your Scale Weight

In my line of work, perhaps the biggest travesty is the perception that a person's worth is defined by waist size or scale weight. All day, every day, I have encounters with remarkable people who have accomplished so much in life and are making amazing contributions to society, but they discount their greatness because they don't fall into the ideal BMI range.

Let's just start with the absurdity of using a nearly two hundred-year-old equation that was devised by a Belgian mathematician (not a physician) to help the government determine how to allocate resources based on whether people were overweight or underweight. It continues to be used by insurance companies and medical practitioners to categorize people by height and weight and define a person's health risks. While this may have been best practice in the 1830s, we now have more sophisticated measurement tools and we know much more about disease predictors independent of weight. Despite mounting criticism about BMI being an archaic measurement that does not take body composition into account, we continue to use a person's BMI as a benchmark for health.

One large-scale study involving an eighteen-year follow-up period looked at incidence of diabetes, coronary heart disease, stroke, and mortality. It showed that obese individuals who met the criteria for normal blood pressure, blood glucose, and cholesterol levels (considered healthy obese) have lower risks for all those conditions than unhealthy subjects regardless of their BMI status. They did have a small increase in risk for future diabetes compared with healthy lean people. With increasing frequency, I'm seeing patients come in who are in the normal weight range according to their BMI, but they were recently diagnosed with prediabetes or diabetes, high cholesterol, or hypertension. This drives home the point that weight is not the only determinant when it comes to health and wellness.

Patients often come in with an idea of what their ideal weight *should* be. I ask them if they've ever been at that weight and if so, when and for how long. Some admit to never being at their "ideal weight" in their adult lives, and others have had brief interludes in their desirable range but only with severe restriction and/or an untenable amount of exercise. I ask instead that they try to imagine what it might be like if they could find their way to a place where they feel strong, confident, and healthy in their bodies without it feeling like a daily struggle. What if they could reject arbitrary, meaningless numbers and let their beautiful bodies do the talking? Which brings us around to a different way of setting up goals and establishing meaningful milestones.

Fat Shaming through the Ages

Not surprisingly, the introduction of the modern-day scale in the late 1800s was what kicked off the omnipresent obsession with weight. We have a long history of drawing conclusions and assigning assumptions about how weight is a predictor of health outcomes. Much of the work that's been done through the Health at Every Size (HAES) program debunks some of the long-held beliefs about direct associations between scale weight and disease.

A research paper published by the HAES group looks at common misconceptions about weight being the sole contributor and primary risk factor for many chronic diseases or modern health concerns. Authors of the paper criticize use of body weight as a target for public health intervention, and instead advocate promoting healthy habits at every size. They point to the psychological toll of weight-biased stigma, and recommend that health-promoting interventions should take into consideration physical, emotional, social, occupational, intellectual, spiritual, and ecological aspects of health.

Ideas that sprung from early Christian beliefs play a leading role in what's now become known as "fat shaming." Biblical references to the sin of gluttony, along with damnation for being too weak to resist temptation, contributed to judgment about what being overweight says about one's character.

Being gluttonous used to be a wealthy person's problem, since food scarcity was a constant reality for those who were less fortunate. Early diet programs were marketed to the more elite members of society who could actually afford to be gluttonous. The privilege of overconsumption reached the masses when food production became more industrialized and cheap and fast food became the norm. Now we talk about the problem of being overfed and undernourished, because eating on a budget often means reliance on highly processed foods or drive-throughs where you can feed a family of four for less than twenty dollars. Shopping for organic foods and grass-fed meat is a luxury reserved for those with heftier paychecks.

At least 85 percent of the patients I see in my practice have BMIs that put them into the overweight or obese category. This might not be surprising, considering 71.6 percent of adults in the United States are overweight or obese according to the Centers for Disease Control. Not to mention that many people who seek help from a dietitian are doing so because they've been told by their doctors that their health problems will vanish if they just lose twenty, thirty, forty-plus pounds.

What's astonishing and heartbreaking to me is that many of these patients have been traumatized by a lifetime of criticism about their weight that includes a lot of inaccurate assumptions made by healthcare providers. I've had tearful patients tell me they stopped going to doctors years ago because they got tired of hearing "you just need to lose weight," without any conversation about what they've tried or what they're currently doing. Not only is it dismissive and judgmental, it's psychologically damaging, and it reinforces the belief that being thinner at any cost is the ultimate goal. I once had a woman tell me that a doctor had told her that God was punishing her by making her overweight.

In defense of physicians, I will say that they don't have nearly enough time with their patients (nor do they have the nutrition education) to engage in diet and behavioral counseling. Many have started referring patients to dietitians and/or counselors to provide guidance to patients who need more support. The entire healthcare (currently the *disease* care) system needs to change so that there's a bigger emphasis on overall wellness and acceptance of all body sizes. There's no place in the system for useless shaming or bullying.

"Years from now, we will look back in horror at the counterproductive ways we addressed the obesity epidemic and the barbaric ways we treated fat people— long after we knew there was a better path."

—Michael Hobbes, *Huffington Post*

We're Already Hard Enough on Ourselves

In a study involving fifty-four females with BMI ranging from 16.94 to 43.89, researchers created avatars of varying body sizes for each participant and asked them to identify which was an accurate representation of their bodies. Women who had BMIs in the normal or underweight categories ranked their body sizes as smaller than their actual size, while women who had BMIs in the overweight or obese categories ranked their body sizes as larger than their actual size. I remember watching a program where there was a lineup of women, all wearing black undergarments, lined up from smallest to largest. Another group of women were asked to choose where they thought they would fit in the lineup. Every single one of them guessed at least two sizes larger than their actual size.

This distorted body image is so prevalent in my practice. People who look to be near average weight are describing themselves as if they are morbidly obese. I've had conversations with some about how they were told they were overweight as children or adolescents and when they look back at pictures from their youth they would never describe themselves as overweight. Or even those who look back at photos from a decade or two decades ago and say, "I can't believe I thought I was fat back then. What I wouldn't give to look like that now!" And so it goes . . . We're so busy constantly chasing the "perfect" body that we never sit in gratitude with the body we have now, which we'll undoubtedly be pining for two decades from now!

Media Influencers and Our Body-Obsessed Culture

It's well known that the media has shaped the way we feel about our bodies over the years. From some of the very first dieting ads, promising a happier, more fulfilling life to those with slimmer figures, to the airbrushed and computer-manipulated photos of impossibly perfect models. And now we have social media to contend with, and the constant exposure to images of celebrities, peers, and acquaintances is making people feel even worse about their bodies. A review of twenty research papers published in 2016 found that social networking positively correlates with body image concerns and disordered eating.

Although there have been some body-positive heroes showing up on the social media scene, the predominant tendency in the fashion and beauty industry is to use images that are not at all representative of what American women look like today. A study published in 2016 sampled measurements of more than 5,500 women in the United States and reported that the average American woman today is between a size 16 and 18 and has an average waist circumference is 37.5 inches. According to the Centers for Disease Control, average height of women is 5'3½", weight is 170.5 pounds, and waist circumference is 38.7 inches. Compare that with the average size of most models, who are generally 5'7" to 5'9" and weigh between 110 and 114 pounds (that's about a size 2, eight full sizes smaller than the average woman!). Runway models tend to be even taller and thinner.

How do we escape the madness? Unless you decide to sequester yourself in the woods or a deserted island with no phones, computers, TVs, or magazines, it's impossible to tune out all the images and messages that we're bombarded with every day. But you can be a wise consumer of media. You can seek out body-positive messages and even cast a vote with your pocketbook by supporting companies that aren't afraid to hire curvy models and/or support philanthropic causes you believe in.

MEDIA FASTING AND PURGING

This is the only context in which I recommend fasting and purging. Use these tips to lessen your exposure to unrealistic imagery and media messaging:

- Take a short break from social media; experiment with not looking at any Facebook, Instagram, or other social media feeds for even one to two days.

- Unsubscribe to magazines that feature underfed, overedited models on the cover.

- Be part of the movement to accept and embrace all body types and sizes. (For more on this, see Resources on page 190.)

Setting Goals with Soul

One of my favorite books by Danielle LaPorte is called *The Desire Map*. She talks about the fundamental flaws of traditional goal setting, which often has us attaching numbers to goals to ensure that they are measurable by most standards. But what's the guarantee when we get to that magic number? If you set a weight goal of 150 pounds, will you immediately feel better, richer, happier, and more complete the day you step on the scale and see those three numbers looking back at you? Research says no. That celebratory moment of reaching your goal is quickly followed by the worry that it won't hold, the wondering if 130 really *is* the magic number, the inevitable feeling that you're still not thin enough, or light enough, or *good enough*.

LaPorte suggests exploring how you want to *feel* as a result of the changes you're making. So instead of saying "I want to weigh 130 pounds," one might say "I want to feel lighter, more agile, flexible, and confident in my body." This is about finding your *why*: Why does any of this matter to you? Making sustainable lifestyle changes is hard enough, but doing it without the investment of your heart and soul makes it an exercise in futility.

When I ask my patients to dig deep and tell me how they want to feel as result of making lifestyle changes, these are a few of the more memorable responses:

· "I want to feel like I belong in my body and my body belongs to me."

· "I want to feel secure and safe in my body."

· "I want to feel like I have a normal relationship with food, where I think about it just enough, but not too much."

· "I want to feel so damn hot that I sign up for those steamy salsa lessons I keep postponing until I lose fifty pounds." (BTW we both decided there was no need to keep waiting and salsa dancing turned out to be the most natural and enjoyable form of exercise *and* she felt *hot* just moving her body to the music.)

- "I want to feel like I can keep up with my grandkids when we're playing at the beach and I want to be around to meet *their* kids."

- "I want to feel strong enough to sign up for a 10K without hesitation and run it without injuring myself."

- "I want to feel like I have the energy to say *yes* to all the fun things I'd like to do in life."

What's Your Why?

Now is the time to find out what really matters to you and identify tangible goals that have meaning to you. This has nothing to do with societal expectations or pressure from your partner, family, friends, or acquaintances. Your *why* belongs only to you. It's not up for scrutiny or debate. It's what motivates you and keeps you connected to your wellness vision. Try this as an uncensored writing activity where you just write the first thing that comes to your mind, and then expand on it until you come up empty. Here are a few prompts to get you started:

- What areas of my life get neglected?

- What activities do I hold back from participating in?

- What brings me deep joy?

- What am I most proud of?

- Am I satisfied with my relationship with my body? If not, how would I like it to be different?

Reflect on your answers and ask yourself again why you want to change your behaviors.

Helpful Hint: If your answers feel like they're lacking substance, keep asking yourself "why?" until you get to a deeper level.

Example:

Q: Why do I want to make these changes?

A: Because I'm tired of feeling like crap.

Q: Why?

A: Because feeling lousy is no fun.

Q: Why?

A: Because pain is a big deterrent.

Q: Why?

A: Because I have to say no to the things I love to do (hiking, skiing, kayaking) because I'm hurting.

Your Why = I want to feel free from pain so that I can say yes to the things I love to do (hiking, skiing, kayaking).

Once you have your *why*, you have some meaningful intel to keep you grounded and connected to your plan. When you're confronted with the usual temptations or you start to fall back into unwanted patterns, you can map against your *why* and immediately feel the incongruence. Incongruence is uncomfortable, so you have to be willing to feel uncomfortable if you choose to ignore your *why*. Conversely, when you're doing things that are aligned with your soul's desire, you feel it in your entire being and you get the internal confirmation that you're doing what's right for you. Can you see how that's different than saying "I need to lose fifty pounds?" Immediately your soul says, "*So what?*"

Vow to Love, Honor, and Respect Your Body

It's time to get serious. I mean, how long have you known this body of yours? How long have you been in a committed relationship together? This is a little like couples counseling in that you have the opportunity to reflect on your role in this relationship and decide if you've been an attentive, caring, compassionate partner and think about whether you can do better. Has your body been putting up with some neglect and abuse that might explain the lack of cooperation? If you feel like there's room for improvement, commit to it. Make a contract with yourself so you remember how serious you want to take this. You get only one body, and you're blessed with it until the end of your time here, so why not make it the healthiest relationship you have? Following is a template for your contract. You can use it as is if it resonates with you or write your own contract if that feels more meaningful. Keep this in a place where you'll be reminded of your vows.

CONTRACT WITH MYSELF

I, _____, do hereby swear to treat my body like a freakin' temple. I understand that I ask a lot of my body all day, every day, and I'm going to make a conscious effort to listen intently to all of the many ways in which my body is trying to communicate with me. I will form a productive partnership with my body and, effective immediately, I will *stop* trying to beat it into submission.

· *I vow to feed myself when I am hungry and to stop eating when I am satisfied (not stuffed).*

· *I vow to rest when my body is tired, resisting the urge to push through.*

· *I vow to move my body in a way that feels pleasing every single day.*

· *I vow to give myself a break from my computer, phone, and TV with the goal of _____ minutes/hours of unplugged rejuvenation every day.*

· *I vow to find something I like about my body and resist the urge to judge and criticize.*

· *I vow to find self-worth in something other than the three numbers I see on the scale (in fact, maybe I vow to ditch the scale altogether!).*

When I'm struggling, and I'm neglecting myself or succumbing to negative or harsh self-talk, I will think of how I find compassion and encouragement from the following beloved people in my life:

_____   _____   _____   _____

I will offer that same kind of compassion and encouragement to myself.

Faithfully,

(your signature)

Make Peace with Your Body

> "To transform anything we must experience it
> fully and love it just the way it is . . .
> Only love transforms."
>
> —*Radical Forgiveness* by Colin Tipping

Step 1: Become aware of your thoughts.

For one full week, pay attention to your thoughts and internal dialogue about your body. Write down the script that is playing out in your head. Try to refrain from any judgment about what's coming up. You are a curious observer of how your mind processes ideas about your body.

Step 2: Examine your thoughts through the lens of compassion.

Review what you've recorded for the week. Notice patterns and habitual thoughts or internal conversations that are on a loop, playing again and again with little reprieve. Are you constantly critiquing or comparing? Do you use harsh or hurtful language? Would you ever say these things to someone you love?

Step 3: Challenge the value and validity of your thoughts.

Challenge each thought with three questions:

1. **Who does this belong to?**
   Often you will find that this is judgment or language that originated from someone else and you've been carrying it around for years or decades.

2. **Does it produce stress, anxiety, or shame?**
   Who wants to listen to a constant replay of something that makes them feel lousy? It's deflating and is most assuredly keeping you trapped in a destructive mindset.

3. **Is there any part that serves me?**
   This would be any aspect of the internal dialogue that is encouraging or empowering. For example, if you hear yourself saying "I have *got* to exercise more," you could evaluate whether exercising more brings something of value to your life—like being able to play with your kids or hike with your partner.

Step 4: Give yourself guidelines.

In order to break old patterns and start creating a better relationship with your body, it's helpful to come up with some guidelines. Much like the bumpers you can use at the bowling alley, these guidelines help keep you moving in the right direction and prevent your mind from falling into the gutter. It can be very liberating to declare what you will no longer tolerate and what you would like to cultivate. Here are a few examples:

I will not *use the three numbers on the scale to define my self-worth.*

I will not *speak disparagingly about my body or anyone else's.*

I will not *compare myself to others.*

I will *start a daily gratitude practice to remind myself of what my body can do.*

I will *look for the things I truly admire in others.*

I will *limit exposure to media that compromises my body confidence.*

Step 5: Find joy in your body.

Forget about forcing yourself to run if you're not a runner or going to the gym if you hate being at the gym. Engage in physical activity that makes you feel joyful. You will build strength and confidence from moving your body in ways that feel pleasing rather than punishing.

- Nature is good for the soul. Look for outdoor activities for every season.

- Make it convenient. If you have to drive forty-five minutes in rush-hour traffic to get to your gym, chances are you won't make it there very often. How about just turning on the music and having a dance party around your living room?

- Be present in your body and notice the sensations that arise and how they change over time. Experience the moment-to-moment bliss of truly inhabiting your body while engaging in an activity you enjoy.

CREATING A DAILY GRATITUDE PRACTICE

Feelings and expressions of gratitude correlate with lower cortisol levels and better hormonal balance in the body. I've noticed that patients who commit to doing a daily gratitude practice are able to turn down the volume on negative self-talk and start to feel better about their bodies. There are a variety of different ways to integrate more gratitude into your life, so it's best to find what resonates with you so that you can make it a regular part of your routine. Consistency is what starts to form new neuronal pathways and allows you to escape the rut of resentment or other unwanted thoughts and feelings.

This generally works best if you choose a time of day (e.g. morning: before you get up, or evening: before dozing off to sleep), then allocate a set period of time (an amount you know you can spare every day) to express your gratitude. Whichever option you choose, try to come up with three things about your body for which you are grateful. In the beginning this might be challenging, and you may have look for basic functions, like "I'm grateful that I can hear the birds singing," or "I'm grateful I can smell my coffee brewing." Over time you will start to see the beauty, not only in how your body functions, but how it shows up in the world. You may find yourself feeling accepting or even proud of parts of your body about which you've felt self-conscious all your life.

Practices to cultivate:

- Daily journal: if you like to write

- Voice recording: if you are too hurried to sit down and write, or if you enjoy listening to audio recordings

- Body scan: if you are a kinesthetic learner, move from head to toe and back again and notice any sensations that arise

- Sticky notes: use obvious visual cues to remind yourself of why you are grateful

- Artistic expression: draw or paint your expression of gratitude

Eat Your Food and Feel Your Feelings

The Hunger Games

What is hunger and how do you identify it? If you're disconnected from your body, it's almost impossible to recognize true physical hunger and distinguish that from something that has nothing to do with your body needing food. We eat for so many different reasons, many of which have nothing to do with actual physical hunger. I've witnessed many epiphanies related to childhood events that firmly planted the seed for a dysfunctional relationship with food. It's time to stop playing a losing game and recognize what you need to feel truly nourished on all levels.

PHYSIOLOGICAL VERSUS EMOTIONAL HUNGER

Physiological hunger is your body's need for fuel. We often override that need so as not to interrupt other pressing matters of the day. The problem is that this creates a metabolic flux from blood sugar instability, hormonal variances, and an urgent need for food at some point. That's why most people report having a dip in energy in the afternoon that generally incites a strong desire for sugar, snack foods, or caffeine. Or all of the above.

If you can learn to better manage the physiological hunger by balancing blood sugar and honoring hunger and satiety cues, emotional eating becomes much easier to identify and correct. Physical or physiological hunger can be described as what we feel from the neck down while emotional hunger is what we feel from the neck up. Thinking that you deserve a treat or a glass of wine because you endured a stressful day is an example of your mind leading the charge.

When we try to make food the answer to all of our problems, we give food more power than it deserves. Food is there to nourish our physical bodies. That's the number-one job of food. When we try to use food to satisfy our soul's desires, we're giving food too big of a job. It's beyond its scope, which is why turning to food to fill an emotional void almost always leads to guilt, shame, or self-loathing.

> **When we try to use food to satisfy our soul's desires, we're giving food too big of a job.**

MANAGING YOUR BODY HUNGER

The first order of business is to establish an eating routine. I'd love to tell you to eat according to your hunger cues, but if you've been skipping meals, going for long periods without eating, or your hormones are out of whack, your hunger cues are probably not super reliable right now. Once you get into a regular, consistent eating routine that you pair with mindful eating, your hunger and satiety cues will be spot-on.

First off, let me just say on the record that I am a believer in breakfast. Every now and again a study will come out that suggests breakfast isn't as important as we thought. I can just tell you from my clinical experience that having patients start the day with a balanced breakfast and incorporate an afternoon snack has done more to cut the cravings and improve energy than any other strategies I have. This works especially well for binge-eating disorders and compulsive overeaters, but it's just a good starting place for most people. I will concede that some people naturally get off to a slower start in the morning. Maybe digestion feels sluggish and appetite is lacking. If that describes you, just experiment with a week or two of having something small, like a half of an avocado, within one or two hours of rising and see if you feel better or worse throughout the day.

One reason that breaking the fast is so important is that your cortisol levels are highest in the morning. That's your fight-or-flight hormone and it's your body's brilliant way of telling you to get out bed and go look for food. It's a primal response, and it's tied to your blood sugar. When you're hypoglycemic your body experiences that as a stressor and your cortisol levels rise. In the morning, eating breakfast is part of what signals your cortisol levels to start lowering. Now here's where I'm bound to lose some people. If you're a coffee drinker, it's best to have coffee with or after your breakfast, *not* before. If you wake up and drink coffee first thing on an empty stomach, you're putting a stimulant in on top of those high cortisol levels and delaying the natural decline of your cortisol curve. Caffeine also messes with your hunger cues and makes you forget that you need breakfast, which may seem like a good thing, but it's not. Reliable hunger cues are a hallmark of a working metabolism. Try eating breakfast within one to two hours of rising and sip on your coffee with your breakfast or enjoy it after.

The other most critical time of day for eating is between lunch and dinner, usually three p.m. for most people. This is the time when blood sugar starts to drop, energy lulls, and concentration begins to fade. It's also when that bowl of candy in the break room starts to call your name. Or when you round up your office mates and head to the coffee shop for venti lattes and pastries. (Side note, I just had a moment of horror when I looked up the Starbucks drink sizes and learned that venti is no longer the largest size! If twenty ounces of sugary coffee isn't enough to get you through the afternoon and keep you up all night, you can supersize that to *thirty-one ounces* with a trenta latte. Ugh!) Bringing a snack from home so that you can sidestep the office junk food landmines and prevent yourself from drowning in a sugary latte can be life-changing.

That afternoon snack can also prevent you from feeling like you're on the brink of starvation and coming in hot at the end of a long day. The two biggest times for mindless eating are late afternoon/early evening (before dinner) and later in the evening (before bed). It just makes good sense to take in more of your nourishment in the first two-thirds of your day when your body needs the energy, and less in the last third of your day when your body is preparing for rest. This is one version of intermittent fasting that I wholeheartedly support.

BREAKFAST IDEAS

- Beauty Bowls (page 112)
- Rainbow Breakfast Bowl (page 104)
- Tofu breakfast scramble (recipe on EatPlayBe.com)
- Avocado toast (on whole grain bread)
- Oatmeal with nuts and berries

SNACK IDEAS

- Mediterranean Snack Platter (page 122)
- Crispy beans and seeds
- Hummus and veggies
- Guacamole and red peppers
- Apple with almond butter
- Marinated baked tofu

A WORD ON INTERMITTENT FASTING

When I'm teaching classes on mindful eating, I'll inevitably get the question, "What do you think about intermittent fasting?" My response is, "I think it's great, and you should do it while you're sleeping." It's true that some research supports intermittent fasting. In one study where subjects confined their eating time to an eight-hour window, there appeared to be a mild decrease in total caloric intake and some weight loss without calorie counting. It may also have some benefit in reducing blood pressure. Other studies show that intermittent fasting has similar benefits to daily caloric restriction.

There are many different options for intermittent fasting, including the 5:2 method, where you restrict to five hundred calories a day for a two days a week; alternate-day fasting, where you limit calories to around five hundred every other day; the twenty-four-hour fast, which is exactly as it sounds; and time-restricted eating, which is the brand that makes the most sense to me. Time-restricted eating means that you have a window of time that you're eating and then stop and let your body rest for twelve to sixteen hours. Basically, this just means that you eat dinner by six thirty or seven, close the kitchen, and don't eat again until one to two hours after you get up in the morning. When people are adhering to this pattern of eating, guess what they're *not* doing—snacking in front of the TV all night right before they're going to be horizontal for eight hours.

I'm not a fan of any of the other types of intermittent fasting, although there are some circumstances where the more extreme forms may be beneficial and can be used as a therapeutic diet plan. For the vast majority of people, trying to avoid food until late in the day, and eating only one or two meals a day creates a psychological hardship and keeps people locked into the restriction/deprivation mindset. It can be isolating and physically punishing (for those who are prone to hypoglycemia, for example), and many people actually end up engaging in binge-type behaviors during the hours they are "allowed" to eat.

Sugar: The Grand Manipulator

While I appreciate the notion of everything in moderation (including moderation), experience tells me that sugar is not so easy to moderate. I refer to sugar as The Grand Manipulator because it influences taste preferences, creates a heightened desire for sweetness, and acts as a neurostimulator. Dr. David Kessler, a board-certified pediatrician and former FDA commissioner, researched the effect of certain food combinations on brain activity and behavior. He eloquently describes his findings in his book *The End of Overeating*, but the gist of it is that the combination of sugar and fat (think ice cream) triggers a dopamine release in the pleasure center of the brain and stimulates the desire for *more, more, more.* Some people are particularly susceptible to this form of neurostimulation, which is why they experience a lust for sugar similar to how addicts would describe their relationship with drugs or alcohol.

When I have patients who confess their love affair with sugar, beating themselves up for lacking the willpower to say no to that second cupcake, I tell them about Dr. Kessler's work. Many breathe a big sigh of relief and are glad to learn that this is not a moral failure or inherent character flaw. It may sound odd, but they take some comfort in knowing that there's a physiological and neurological explanation for their unreasonably strong cravings. I think it's also helpful to understand the facts about this particular ingredient.

FACTS ABOUT SUGAR CONSUMPTION

- The average American now consumes about 150 pounds of sugar per year, which equates to three pounds or six cups in one week

- Most processed foods in the United States contain added sugar

- Excess sugar is stored as fat in the body

- There is ample evidence to suggest that sugar could increase the risk of heart disease, diabetes, and cancer

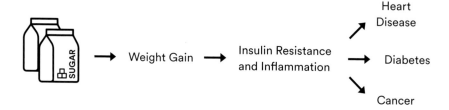

A FEW MORE REASONS NOT TO EAT SUGAR

- Sugar suppresses the immune system

- Sugar can elevate triglycerides and lead to high cholesterol

- Sugar offsets the minerals in your body

- Sugar feeds cancer cells and can promote tumor growth

- Sugar may contribute to osteoporosis

- Sugar may contribute to headaches and migraines

- Sugar may promote hormonal imbalances and worsen PMS

BENEFITS OF LIMITING SUGAR

- Your palate adjusts to enjoy foods that are less sweet
- Your blood sugar regulates
- Your mood is more stable and concentration improves
- Your energy is more authentic and consistent
- It's easier to lose and maintain weight
- Your cravings diminish

INGREDIENTS TO AVOID (READ INGREDIENT LISTS ON FOOD LABELS)

- High-fructose corn syrup
- Sugar
- Sucrose
- Evaporated cane juice
- Artificial sweeteners (sucralose, aspartame, etc.)

SUGAR ALTERNATIVES

- Honey
- Pure maple syrup
- Stevia
- Agave nectar
- Coconut palm sugar
- Monk fruit sugar

Kick the Craving and Change the Habit

There's no one-size-fits-all strategy to liberate yourself from sugar cravings. For some people (those who are more susceptible to the dopamine hit), abstinence may be necessary. For others, eating sweet treats mindfully will be enough to self-regulate. Regardless, I think ditching the sugar for a few weeks can help provide some much-needed clarity around your thoughts, attitudes, and behaviors toward food. The best part is that most people start feeling more balanced with fewer cravings within one short week of detoxing from sugar. It's not to say that you'll fly by those donuts in the break room without so much as a second look, but you probably won't feel quite so vulnerable to the seductive powers of sugar. And although you're likely to notice a difference within the first week of this experiment, I recommend that you carry on for three weeks (new habits are more likely to form with twenty-one days of practice).

CLEAR THE CRAP

- Do a kitchen clean-out and get rid of sugary junk food.
- Restock your fridge and pantry with beautiful, colorful, fresh food.
- Empty your desk drawers of candy and put a fresh fruit bowl on your desk (fill it with apples or clementines).

BALANCE YOUR BODY

Physiological craving = the body's need for fuel

- Start the day with a savory breakfast (e.g., tofu veggie scramble or egg and veggie frittata).
- Avoid going more than four hours without eating (an afternoon snack is particularly helpful).
- Include a complex carb in at least two of your three meals (e.g., ½ cup quinoa or brown rice, 3 to 4 fingerling potatoes, ½ of a baked yam)—this prevents you from feeling carb starved.
- Eat slowly, savoring each bite and allowing your mind, body, and spirit to know that you are satiated.
- If the craving comes, turn your attention to naturally sweet foods like fruit or vegetables (e.g., carrots, beets, yams, sugar snap peas).
- Curb your cravings with a big bite of kraut. The beneficial bacteria in fermented foods send signals to the brain that can help turn off the urge for sugar.
- Close the kitchen after dinner and give your body a well-deserved rest.

CHANGE YOUR MIND

- Ask yourself how you feel in this moment and name the feeling—maybe the feeling doesn't need to be fed, just acknowledged.
- Scan your body and notice any areas that are calling for attention. Send breath, love, and light to those areas and see if you can perceive a shift.
- Fact-check negative thoughts and harsh judgments about yourself and others.
- Try hypnotherapy or tapping (Emotional Freedom Technique, EFT), also referred to as psychological acupressure.

"THAT'S NOT FOR ME."

I had a patient who was a lifelong dieter and very committed to ditching the dieting mentality and becoming a mindful, intentional eater. She quickly embraced the practice of engaging her senses and slowing down while eating and was amazed that she was capable of feeling truly satiated. We talked a lot about the power of the mind and the importance of eating with intention. After the first couple of visits, she came back and reported that there were lots of goodies lying around at work (not a new problem), but she had come up with a strategy that was working beautifully for her.

"When I see junky food that I know I don't really want to be eating I say to myself, 'That's not for me,'" she explained. "When I say it, something clicks in my brain and I can just bypass the internal struggle." I asked if she felt deprived or angry about walking away from these foods.

"No. It just makes things very clear to me," she responded.

I was intrigued by her use of such a simple mantra so I shared it with other patients who were having similar challenges. Much to my surprise, those four magic words worked equally well for many of them. Try it for yourself or come up with your own mantra that allows you to have clarity about your food choices.

THE REST IS IN YOUR HEAD (AND YOUR HEART)

Once you restore the physiological balance in your body and find the eating pattern and combinations of foods that work best for you, and reduce the amount of sugar you're eating, cravings will likely decrease significantly. When you're perpetually well nourished, what you're left with is no longer physical hunger; it's emotional hunger. This includes eating to fill a void, like lack of joy or love, or it could be eating as an attempt to numb yourself from unpleasant feelings, like anxiety or sadness. It can also be using food as a reward, which is a learned pattern that typically comes from your family food culture growing up.

In fact, there are many emotional eating habits we get exposed to throughout our childhood that present themselves as coping mechanisms. For my patients who grew up in environments of abuse or neglect, food may have been the only coping mechanism they knew, and it served an important purpose when they needed it. With the development of a wider variety of effective coping skills, it's safe to let go of the ones that no longer feel healthy or helpful. This is where therapy can be extremely useful and is often a great adjunct to nutrition counseling.

I find that group sessions are particularly helpful for my patients who are struggling with emotional eating. The support they get from others who have similar stories is invaluable. The following chart is one that was born out of one of the first group sessions I ran to help people change their relationships with food. I stood at the whiteboard and asked them to identify emotional triggers for eating. They shouted out all of those you see listed in the chart, and then we brainstormed ideas for nonfood responses to those emotional triggers. Experiment with some of these ideas or come up with a list of your own to try.

PHYSICAL HUNGER

Symptom	Remedy
Hunger (experienced below the neck); stomach is growling; blood sugar is low; feeling of emptiness in the stomach	Food

EMOTIONAL HUNGER

Access/Abundance	Eat mindfully and with intention; keep triggering foods out of the home
Anxiety	Exercise; practice deep breathing; meditate; recite affirmations
Boredom	Recognize and allow or embrace boredom; read a book; volunteer; be active; rest; nap; meditate
Control (lack of or need to)	Give it up to the universe; examine the need for control; identify elements of life that feel "out of control"; refer to serenity prayer*
Depression	Exercise; get counseling; look for mind/body imbalance; journal; read *Unstuck* by Dr. James Gordon; enjoy nature; get acupuncture

* *"Grant me the serenity to accept the things I cannot change, courage to change the things I can, and wisdom to know the difference."*

Symptom	Remedy
Fear	Talk with trusted friend/family member; pray; meditate; identify irrational thought patterns; set goals
Grief	Go to grief counseling; reach out for support from friends/family; accept emotional expression; cry; scream
Loneliness	Connect with friends; volunteer in the community; spend time with a pet; get touch therapy (e.g., massage)
Restlessness	Exercise/release it; identify the source
Reward/Praise	Identify nonfood forms of reward; have a spa day; travel; go on a weekend getaway; get a pedicure; see a movie; take a bath; have time to self
Self-Loathing	Practice forgiveness and acceptance; speak or write affirmations; replace negative thoughts with positive/empowering thoughts; journal; use nurturing language
Stress	Meditate; pray; practice deep breathing; have spa time; talk with friends/family members; simplify and learn to say no; eliminate the stressor; exercise

THE STORY OF KAREN

Karen was a forty-year-old mother of nine-month-old twins who was concerned that she was putting on weight despite breastfeeding. She admitted to having a history of severe sugar cravings that had become even more prominent, and she had a history of disordered eating in her twenties. Her time and energy were limited as a new mom, and she was concerned about her ability to stick to a plan. When she indulged in something sweet, she would say, "Well, now the whole day is shot," and would continue to binge on sugar, then crash and feel lethargic.

I talked to Karen about the importance of eating nourishing foods at regular intervals to keep her blood sugar more balanced throughout the day. We came up with some foods that were easy to prepare, foods that sounded good to Karen. I also suggested starting the day with a savory breakfast, which generally really helps curb persistent sugar cravings.

At the second visit, Karen had been very consistent with the savory breakfast. "I'm surprised how much of a difference that has made," she said. "And I unintentionally shortened my window of time to binge on sweets so I really haven't been binging." She was disappointed in a lack of weight loss in the two weeks since our first visit, but was feeling better overall.

We talked about including more complex carbs in her diet, like quinoa, brown rice, yams, potatoes, and beans. I also encouraged her to make no apologies for taking shortcuts when it came to food prep. If ever there was a time in her life when she should be able to get away with buying precut veggies, this was it!

When Karen came back a few weeks later she had gone on a trip with family, fell back into some of her old food habits (which is easy to do around family), and her sweet tooth came back with a vengeance. We talked about finding her "why" and I encouraged her to ask herself what she values about the way she shows up in the world. We also talked about coming up with nonfood rewards, defined as things that would feed her soul. She was interested in gardening and art, so she talked about outings to the nursery and learning more about artwork that was displayed in her building.

A couple of weeks later, Karen was happy to report that she was able to get right back on track. She was doing the savory breakfast every day, and came up with the idea of "casting a vote" for the type of eater she wanted to be every time she made a choice about food. She had finished weaning the twins and her appetite had declined, so she was naturally feeling compelled to eat less. Before she left my office, I reminded her, "Food is there to nourish your physical body. It can't feed your soul, entertain you when you're bored, comfort you when you're sad—that's too big of a job for food." I encouraged her to keep working on her list of things that really feed her soul.

The last time she came in she was getting ready to return to work. She felt like she had established some habits that were really sticking, and her cravings had subsided significantly. "It feels very freeing to not feel as sugar addicted," Karen told me. She was surprised about how her wellness priorities had shifted. "When I first came in, I would have told you that losing weight was my number-one priority and anything less would have been disappointing," she said. "Even though I haven't lost a lot of weight yet, I now understand how freeing it can be to feel like I'm not beholden to sugar cravings and to not constantly obsess about food. I know the weight will come off eventually and I just feel healthier overall." She was still working on figuring out what her new routine would be when she went back to work, but she was going in with confidence, more energy, and a resolve to nourish herself with intention.

Eat Like You Mean It

Benefits of Mindful Eating

- Reduces binge eating and emotional eating
- Improves digestion
- Increases satisfaction and satiety
- Acts as an innate form of portion control
- Leads to more sustainable weight loss
- Creates a healthier relationship with food
- Generates body awareness and acceptance
- Honors body wisdom

Number-one reason to eat mindfully: *it makes eating more enjoyable!*

SIT. BREATHE. SEE. SMELL. TASTE. CHEW. SAVOR. ENJOY.

A few years ago, I went to a Vipassana ten-day silent meditation retreat. Once I had committed, almost blindly I might add, I started reading through the information about what to expect on this journey to enlightenment. What really caught my attention was that we would be served vegan meals (fine by me!), and we would eat only two meals a day, breakfast and lunch. One could enjoy tea and fruit in the evening if desired (I think that's how they put it in the course description). I panicked. I'm a person who eats five to six times a day, so this was bringing up food insecurities, concerns about my health and well-being, worries about blood sugar plummeting, and maybe even fainting spells from starvation. My mind was creating some pretty bizarre scenarios, and I even contemplated having one of my doctor friends write a note so that I could be allowed snacks. Oddly, I didn't spend any time thinking about how difficult it would be to sit in meditation for ten hours a day for ten days straight without talking to a soul. This tells you how food obsessed I really was!

When I arrived onsite the first night, we were allowed to talk to our fellow Vipassana companions and get acquainted with our roommates. My roommate was from Colorado and also seemed to be worried about the food situation, but in a very different way. She put a big bottle of Tums on our bathroom counter and told me I could help myself. "I hear the menu has a lot of roughage, so we might need these," she told me. I didn't have the heart to tell her this is the way I eat at home and having someone else cook this kind of food for me was a dream come true. I just thanked her and smiled.

Every morning there was a serve-yourself oatmeal bar, which consisted of a huge pot of oatmeal and a row of small bowls of nuts, seeds, dried fruit, sweeteners like honey and brown sugar, milk alternatives, and bananas. We were to dish up our oatmeal, choose our toppings, and sit in the dining hall in noble silence (meaning you also refrain from staring people down while not talking to them). We had one hour from when they would strike the breakfast gong to the time we were to report to the meditation hall. The first day I finished my oatmeal in ten minutes and then walked around in circles in the rain for fifty minutes, probably planning my escape. As the days wore on, I became proficient at savoring that bowl of oatmeal for almost an entire hour. I took my time making very deliberate choices with my toppings, I roamed about until I found the perfect spot looking out into the meadow where the deer were grazing. I set my place and gave thanks to the many people who were volunteering their time to create this whole experience for us. And then I ate . . . so. very. slowly. I really had no idea you can keep oatmeal in your mouth for that long. I can still recall the texture of the oats, peanut butter, and banana on my tongue, and I can smell the fresh ground peanut butter. I can hear the person next to me chewing louder than I liked. I remember how comforting it felt to have that morning routine.

By the way, my food scarcity fears were completely unwarranted and went away by the second day, when I realized that your energy requirements go down pretty significantly when you're just sitting in meditation for most of your day. I learned many valuable lessons, not the least of which was that, if I could eat oatmeal for an entire hour, I sure as hell could sit down and savor my breakfast for fifteen minutes in the morning before work.

Thoughts on Intuitive Eating

There are a variety of different views on intuitive eating. One school of thought says your body will self-regulate as long as you're not imposing any restrictions. So if you feel like eating ice cream, *dig in*! Keep eating until you no longer have the urge. But what if you just don't lose the urge? In fact, maybe the urge just keeps getting stronger. While I'm a fan of the concept of intuitive eating, I worry that our food supply has become so highly processed and sugar laden that we're being manipulated by ingredient combinations that keep us forever craving and never feeling satisfied.

The other challenge with intuitive eating is that a body that is overfed and undernourished does not produce reliable hunger and satiety cues, so succumbing to the craving of the moment because your mind tells you that your body wants and deserves it is not the same as feeling the sensory experience of hunger and feeding yourself accordingly. You can definitely get to a place where you can trust that the cues you're receiving are legitimate, but if you're engaging in mindless eating and binge-like behaviors, the reliability factor is pretty compromised.

Energy Flows Where Intention Goes

I like to describe mindful eating as *intentional* eating. And this way of eating will become more *intuitive* after the body restores itself to its natural homeodynamic state. Eating with intention requires some planning and preparation, but the payoff is huge and you'll quickly discover that as you begin to eliminate the power struggle with food. You'll feel your energy improve, your mind will become clear and focused, your body will feel lighter and more agile. Planning and prep become less cumbersome as you start feeling better and the benefits of your work become abundantly clear.

If you're struggling with fatigue or low energy you may have to fake it 'til you make it. Set up the structure, stick to the plan, and trust that you'll end up with more fuel in the tank to further your journey down the road to wellness. You can also take shortcuts with no apologies. There are plenty of ways in which you can get nourishing food in front of you, even if you don't have the energy to do a lot of food prep and cooking. There are lots of precut veggies now in the produce section, some decent frozen meals with recognizable ingredients, natural foods markets with salad bars and healthy deli options, meal delivery services, and even personal chef options if you have the financial resources. Don't let an energy deficit or lack of enthusiasm about cooking stop you from becoming the mindful, intentional eater you deserve to be.

Consider for a moment how much we require and expect from our bodies. We want to maintain a healthy weight, be active, have good energy, feel sexy, be productive, have good digestion, have a strong immune system, think clearly, sleep well, and wake up energized every morning. Now ask yourself how much you're willing to put into the system to realize those expectations. Is it reasonable to expect complete cooperation from your body if you're unable to find the time to simply feed yourself regularly and with intention throughout the day?

I get that we're overscheduled and overcommitted and there are *never* enough hours in the day. But now might be the time to evaluate with brutal honesty what has to give in order for you to be able to form a more productive partnership with your body and put enough energy into the system to get the returns you so badly desire.

Learn to Say No

I had the great fortune of working with a functional medicine doctor named Jack Kornberg, who spent many years as a board-certified surgeon before he got tired of patching up problems that could have been prevented with simple lifestyle changes. Dr. Jack made the radical decision to leave the lucrative world of surgical intervention behind him and came to work at the Functional Medicine Research Center. He would see patients with complex issues and come up with a customized lifestyle prescription, and I would support those recommendations with more in-depth nutritional coaching.

One day a patient came into my office looking fairly stunned after seeing Dr. Jack. I asked Jessica what was on her mind. "Well, I just got a prescription from the good doctor," she said. "I was telling him about all of the obligations in my life and discussing the challenge to find time to make the necessary changes to my diet." She handed me a slip that came from Dr. Jack's very official-looking prescription pad. There were just three words in very large, bold letters . . . JUST SAY NO!

Those words were life-changing for Jessica. She had an autoimmune condition that we thought was the main contributor to her chronic fatigue. As it turned out, her constant efforts to *do everything* and *be everything* were the biggest drain on her energy and were ultimately triggering many of the symptoms of her autoimmune condition. Once she had permission (and not just permission, but a *prescription* from her beloved doctor) to stop taking on the weight of the world, her condition improved dramatically.

Not surprising, saying no to some of the less critical obligations in her life gave Jessica the time and space to be able to take better care of herself. She asked her partner for help with meal planning and shopping. She got her two kids involved in Sunday food prep and they all started eating better as a result. Jessica's energy continued to improve and she was able to do some light exercise for the first time in years. Even her labs started looking better with a decrease in her autoimmune markers.

"I feel like I've come home to my body," said Jessica. "I didn't realize how often I would override my basic needs to try to be the woman who could do it all. Now I realize that when I don't intentionally make time to care for *me*, my body protests loudly and everyone I care about suffers because I can't function. Talk about a wake-up call!"

I see this all the time with my patients. If I had a dollar for every time I hear the phrase "I know what I'm supposed to do, I just can't seem to find the time to do it," I'd be able to retire. A perceived lack of time is the number-one obstacle to success. Intentional living means that you recognize there are limits to what you can accomplish in a day and the highest priority every day is to take care of your mind, body, and spirit.

Creating Space in Your Schedule

If the activities you need to engage in to be healthy and well keep getting usurped by other responsibilities, it's time to put on your project-manager hat and get to work on creating a more realistic schedule. Very often, this means saying no because there simply aren't enough hours in the day to accomplish everything and take good care of yourself. Sometimes it just means that you ask for help from family and friends. Use the following questions so you can start to really prioritize your daily, weekly, and monthly activities. Make sure you have access to all the tools you use to keep track of your obligations. Although schedules vary from week to week, use a typical week and go day by day to answer the following questions.

1. How much scheduled time do you have in each day?

2. How much unscheduled time do you have each day? How is that time generally spent?

3. Which scheduled activities must be fulfilled with no alterations? (e.g., you must be at work by eight a.m. Monday through Friday.)

4. Which scheduled activities are flexible and can be modified in some way? (e.g., shuttling kids around to ten different activities, volunteering, socializing)

5. Do you have any self-care activities scheduled? (e.g., exercise, food prep, therapy, massage, bedtime ritual, etc.)

6. How much time to you spend on self-care activities in a given week? Is that enough time to feel like you're being consistent and getting the results you deserve?

7. What's one thing you could take off your daily, weekly, and monthly schedule to create more space? What's one thing you're doing now that could be delegated?

Next steps:

· Unscheduled time is important, and you should strive to have some un-scheduled time every day that can be filled with restorative activities like meditation, reflection, gardening, or just simply being instead of doing.

· Commit to removing some flexible scheduled activities. You can think of this as a temporary experiment, where you have the option to resume some of these activities at a later date when your schedule allows.

· Schedule your high-priority wellness activities, starting with the well-ness activities that will have the biggest impact on your mental and phys-ical health. Resist filling every minute of unscheduled time with self-care activities.

Did You Inherit Your Mother's Eating Habits?

Often it's helpful to have a better understanding of where your beliefs and behaviors around food and eating came from. Sometimes it's obvious, like "Grandma gave me cookies every time I was feeling bad." Other times the origins of your eating patterns are a little tougher to tease out. Suffice it to say that some of the unwanted behaviors you're engaging in are learned behaviors and it may be easier to let go of the ones that are not serving you so well if you can simply acknowledge where they came from. If you used food for comfort, there may have been a very good reason. Perhaps that was the best (or only) coping mechanism you had at the time.

EATING DISORDER VERSUS DISORDERED EATING

An eating disorder is defined as an illness that is characterized by severe disturbances in eating behaviors and related thoughts and emotions. The three most common types of eating disorders are anorexia, bulimia, and binge-eating disorder. There are many different ways to have a dysfunctional relationship with food outside the diagnosis of a full-on eating disorder.

Many of my patients exhibit disordered-eating patterns that often stem from a lifetime of dieting, food scarcity as a child, or shame and guilt around food and eating. So when people confess that they're a "closet eater," or they binge every night after a long day at work, or they restrict calories and obsessively track their intake, I know that they'll benefit from making some changes to how they eat while subtly starting to shift their mindset about what constitutes perpetual self-nourishment.

Creating Your Own Food Culture

Exciting news! Part of this process is that you get to design your own family food culture. This is an opportunity to unpack some of the baggage that came from all the influencers from your past. You get to decide which food and eating habits you want to permanently release and what traditions you'd like to keep. You also get to consider what a supportive food environment will look like for you and your family. Ask yourself these key questions:

· Who are the people who currently influence, or *are influenced by*, my food choices?

· What would I like to change about my food environment at home?

· What's the first step I can take to make that change happen in my home?

· What would I like to change about my food/eating behaviors outside of the home?

· What's one step I can take to make that change happen outside my home?

Discovering the Remedy to Hunger (a.k.a. Eating)

Remember the contract you made with yourself in Stop the Struggle (page 43)? Well this an extension of that with an emphasis on the mindful eating part. When it comes to self-nourishment, you have the innate sensibility to figure out when it's time to feed yourself. You were born with that ability. You've just spent a lifetime trying to ignore or override it. Now let's experiment with the opposite of trying to beat your body into submission. Like any healthy, nonabusive relationship, this requires listening with a keen ear (and in this case "listening" also means feeling), asking questions, honoring your body wisdom and intuition, and responding accordingly.

Here's an example:

DYSFUNCTIONAL RELATIONSHIP WITH YOUR BODY

Body: *I've woken up feeling tired and hungry.*

Mind: I need coffee—let's wait to eat until at work.

Body: *I'm still tired—coffee is kicking in, and now my hunger is on hold.*

Mind: There's lots to do this morning—I've hit the ground running at work—so I need more coffee.

Body: *I'm overstimulated—my hunger is still on hold.*

Mind: How did it get to be one o'clock? I should hunt for food.

Body: *Feed me! I need a quick hit of glucose to stay alert and functioning.*

Mind: Maybe I'll grab something from the food truck—something fried and carby sounds good! I'll eat healthy tomorrow.

Body: *I'm feeling heavy, full, tired, bloated, foggy.*

Mind: I need to push through the day—maybe some caffeine or sugar will help.

Body: *I'm tired, yet overstimulated—hoping for some real nourishment sometime soon.*

Mind: It's time to head home—but I haven't really planned for dinner. Maybe I'll get take out or throw something together—I'm exhausted.

Body: *I'm exhausted, nutrient deprived, and dehydrated.*

Mind: Why am I still hungry? Maybe a glass of wine will help me relax. I can't resist this ice cream . . . or these chips . . . or this chocolate—Hey! What's happening on Facebook? Maybe we'll just watch one episode of that new Netflix series. . . .

Body: *Ugh! I give up!*

PRODUCTIVE PARTNERSHIP WITH YOUR BODY

Body: *I've woken up slowly and have started to feel hungry.*

Mind: Good morning, body! Enjoy a good stretch and contemplate breakfast.

Body: *I've gently gotten into the rhythm of the morning.*

Mind: I'll pull together a balanced breakfast, relax, and savor this first meal.

Body: *I'm feeling grateful and nourished, with increasing energy and mental clarity—ready to take on the day!*

Mind: What a productive morning! It's midday and I'm feeling the sensation of hunger. I'll take a break now, move away from my distractions, and eat a satisfying meal.

Body: *I'm happy to have some midday sustenance—energy feels stable, concentration is good.*

Mind: Here comes that midafternoon slump! I'll get up and move my body, breathe, and eat a balanced snack.

Body: *There's no need for a nap now! I have plenty of energy to get through the rest of the day—more movement would feel good after a day of sitting!*

Mind: There's always more to be done, but it's time to wrap up my tasks for the day and check in with my body to see what kind of movement would feel best.

Body: *Oooh! A walk feels magnificent! I feel the warmth of the sun on my face and the cool breeze dancing over my skin. I feel connected to the earth and I'm reminded that I'm part of a bigger universe.*

Mind: I'm noticing subtle signs of hunger and am ready to mindfully prepare our final meal of the day. I give myself permission to make something simple and light yet nourishing, and I've made the time to relax into meal preparation without haste and with deep gratitude.

Body: *I'm feeling satisfied, not stuffed—completely content and ready to wind down in preparation to rest after a long, busy day. Zzzzz.*

EATING LIKE AN ASSH*LE

Jim came to me with a desire to lose weight and a healthy dose of skepticism that anything I would say could produce the kind of results he was seeking. He recounted his last appointment with his primary care physician, who Jim had asked to run a complete battery of tests. Jim was convinced that something must be "off" for him to gain weight so easily and to have such a hard time losing it. When the doctor got the test results, he reviewed them with Jim. "Well Jim, I think I understand what your problem is," said the doctor. "I knew it! Did something show up on my labs?" asked Jim. "No. Your labs are all within normal range. I think your problem is that you eat like an asshole," replied the doctor. Now that might offend a great number of patients, but Jim is not one of them. "You know he's right," Jim told me. "I do eat like an asshole. I binge on sugary foods or whatever I can find and I treat my body like I don't give a shit." Jim and I had a lot of discussions about finding the motivation to really want to make the changes that were necessary to shed the weight for good. He had a growing interest in converting to a plant-based diet, so he signed up for a vegan meal kit delivery service, which rekindled his interest in cooking. Jim continues to work on prioritizing self-care and balancing that with a very demanding job, but I think his doctor would agree that he no longer eats like an asshole.

Settling into the Sacred Act of Eating

Being a mindful eater takes practice. If you're used to multitasking all the time, and you never or rarely just sit and eat, this may feel like a colossal waste of time at first. Allow it to be whatever it needs to be and just notice how you're feeling, without judgment. Be curious about your interaction with food and your ingrained eating habits.

Here's an activity to get you started. This is a way to really amplify the act of mindful eating and reflect on how the experience was for you. You can do this on your own, or try it with a partner, friend, or family member(s).

MINDFUL EATING ACTIVITY

- Create a beautiful, healthy meal made from foods you love to eat.
- Set the table with linens, candles, whatever you have that makes it feel like a special meal.
- Arrange the food onto your plate and sit comfortably in your dining chair.
- Notice the way the food looks on your plate.
- Pay attention to the aromas and notice whether you can pick up on the fragrances of individual ingredients.
- Take the first bite and really tune into the texture and flavors. Try to chew slowly and notice how the food changes as you chew.
- Notice the sensations in your body as you swallow.
- Eat the rest of your meal in this mindful way, engaging all of your senses.

After the meal, answer these questions:

1. What was the best part about my mindful eating experience?
2. What was the most challenging part?
3. How does this differ from how I normally eat?

Sitting in the Suck

I was running a twelve-week group program on mindful eating and after setting the stage with an interactive demonstration on how to mindfully eat a piece of chocolate, I gave the group their homework. I asked that they go home and practice sitting at the table with no other distraction, no phone or computer at the table, no TV running in the background, and focus only on the sacred act of eating. I gave them a mindful eating tip sheet and suggested that they follow these instructions:

· Fix a plate and sit at the table.

· Remove other distractions.

· *Breathe* and relax into your seat.

· Look at the food and allow yourself to salivate.

· Engage your senses and eat slowly, putting the fork down between bites.

· Savor and enjoy.

I imagined this as a revolutionary activity that everyone would quickly come to appreciate as the most desirable way to eat. The next week I opened the meeting with a check-in and asked people to share their experiences with the mindful eating activity. One of the participants, who was known for her quick wit and devilish sense of humor, raised her hand enthusiastically. "Yes, Lori! I'm eager to hear how it went for you," I said.

"Well, I did exactly what you asked," said Lori. "I sat at the table by myself because my husband was out of town. I put my phone in another room so I wouldn't be tempted. And I just focused on the business of eating. And after a couple of bites, I said to myself . . . *this sucks*!" The room went quiet and then many of the others started laughing and nodding. "I mean, I felt lonely and extremely bored and kind of pathetic, really," she went on. "But I stuck with it anyway because, well hell! I'm no quitter! And I just told myself, Lori, you're going to have to *sit in the suck*."

So Lori sat in the proverbial suck for nearly every meal for the entire week. "Okaaay . . . then what happened?" I asked, with cautious optimism. "Oh well it started to suck less," stated Lori, like it was the most obvious thing in the world. "And in fact, I started to understand why it could be a good thing to be less distracted while eating. I mean, I definitely knew when I was done," said Lori. "And I have to admit that I ate less. And for the first time in months, weight started coming off and I wasn't even trying. So that certainly helped to keep me motivated. And I can't say that I *love* mindful eating yet. It still kinda sucks some of the time. But I guess I'm optimistic that it will just keep sucking less if I keep doing it until it just becomes a habit."

I've recounted this story numerous times to patients who came back after a few weeks of trying mindful eating and noting that it was harder than expected or they felt very emotional, vulnerable, or just plain bored. Lori's story helps them understand that it's normal to be uncomfortable with undistracted eating in the beginning. You're just not trained to do it and our culture doesn't support it, so naturally it feels like you're going against the grain. Try to commit to "sitting in the suck" for at a least a couple of weeks before you throw your arms up in defeat.

Reconnecting with the Joy of Gathering, Preparing, and Eating Good Food

If we could suspend diet-fueled beliefs, worries, and concerns about food and relish the very personal, individualized art of feeding ourselves and our loved ones, we would be much happier for it. One good way to stop the struggle and start changing your mindset is to travel. Our Western food culture celebrates eating rapidly while multitasking and encourages spending minimal time on gathering and preparing food. How else will we find those extra hours in the day for screen time?

But this is not the case in much of the rest of the world. In many developing countries, meal preparation occupies the vast majority of the day. When resources are scarce, and you're relying on what the land and/or sea provide, food is nothing short of a miracle of nature. It's valued for its life-giving properties and never taken for granted. Food gathering is a daily event and food preparation is a shared responsibility. Treasured recipes are passed along from generation to generation, not on a note card or in an email, but through the hands-on experience of cooking together.

When I was thirty-two, I traveled to Turkey on a business trip for the PR firm I was working for at the time. My client was the Hazelnut Council (Turkey is the world's number-one hazelnut producer), and my team and I were there to learn about all things hazelnut. We visited growers, processing plants, and food manufacturers, and we ate *a lot* of hazelnuts. But we also got to fully experience the Turkish food culture. Most memorable was a midday meal on a day that we were driving through the hazelnut-growing region along the Black Sea. We stopped at a charming restaurant with a beautiful terrace overlooking the sea. As we were seated, a man with a fishing pole appeared on the rocks beneath us and cast his line out into the water. Within minutes he was reeling in a good-size fish, which our guide explained would be part of our lunch. I had never tasted fish that was so fresh and perfectly prepared. Each dish that was served featured local ingredients that had been procured that morning. Every bite was a representation of the small town we were visiting, and the experience was unforgettable.

My travels to Europe, Mexico, Indonesia, and Central America have given me the gift of perspective on food and eating. What I witnessed was a deep respect and appreciation for the food that the land provides and a certain pride in the preparation that appears to be mostly absent in our American food culture.

Consider the slow food movement, which was started in 1986 by an Italian food and wine journalist named Carlo Petrini. The slow food movement was born out of a desire to reject the ever-growing industrialization of our world food supply and reconnect with the simple joy of eating foods that are grown and prepared with love and attention. The whole goal is to *slow down*, savor, and enjoy. Founders of the movement strive to protect local and regional food traditions and never lose sight of the "gastronomic pleasures of food." Supporters are keen on enlightening people about the importance of food biodiversity and the impact that our food decisions have on the planet.

First-World Food Gathering:
Confessions of a Spoiled Shopper

I have a dirty little secret. I *hate* grocery shopping. I don't like being in brightly lit stores, roaming the aisles with dozens of other hangry shoppers who clearly do not understand grocery cart etiquette! I also dislike looking for obscure ingredients that do not have an obvious category that would be listed on the grocery aisle signs overhead. Oh, and I should mention that I'm plagued with the inexplicable resistance to asking personnel for help. So, shopping has historically been a weekly chore that would fill me with dread.

But then I was thumbing through a little book called *How to Eat* by Thich Nhat Hanh, which is about minute-to-minute mindfulness in every aspect of eating, including food gathering. And the simple line "we get to choose" really resonated with me. In fact, the very next time I went to the market I was standing in the produce section of my favorite local co-op, surrounded by a stunning selection of fruits and veggies and I started to tear up. It hit me like a ton of bricks. "I get to choose," I said under my breath. I have an abundance of healthy, fresh, colorful, food that I can put in my basket, pay for, and take home to create a meal that will nourish my body and satisfy my senses. How lucky am I? It would be a travesty not to notice this good fortune every time I step into a grocery store.

This realization completely transformed my thinking and brought me into a place of immense gratitude. Don't get me wrong, I'm still strategic about when to shop to avoid the checkout line traffic jam and other unpleasant features of shopping, but I no longer dread it and I also find myself engaging more with my local produce guy and even striking up conversations with fellow shoppers on occasion. I—we—get to choose.

GROCERY SHOPPING WITH GRATITUDE

Choose your time wisely: Look at your calendar and find a time when you can afford to spend thirty to forty-five minutes at the grocery store without feeling rushed. If you dislike shopping with the masses, avoid the hours of five to eight p.m. on weeknights and midday on weekends.

Pull up in peace: As you drive into the parking lot, try to leave behind any lingering stress. Imagine that you are literally driving away from life's stressors and pulling into the parking lot of peace. Once you've found your spot, turn off the car and have a quiet moment to yourself. Breathe and feel the muscles in your body relax.

TIP: If you've got kiddos in the car, play the old "let's see how long we can be quiet before we get out of the car" game.

Enter with awe: As you walk into your little food emporium, take a moment to notice a few of the things that you would normally overlook: the displays in the front of the store, the uniformity of the rows of groceries, the music playing overhead—just notice.

Make produce your priority: Head to the produce section first and notice the many choices of fresh, plant-based foods. Have fun with your selections. Notice what's in season, new arrivals, unfamiliar fruits or veggies. Be bold and challenge yourself or your kiddos to choose one new thing to try.

Check yourself at checkout: As you approach the checkout line, notice what's coming up for you. Are you looking for the shortest line? Getting irritated with the chatty checker? Turn your attention to the sensations in your body and see if you can quiet your mind. Give yourself the space to feel genuine gratitude for the ability to purchase this nourishing food for you and your family.

FOOD PREP WITH PEP

Out with the old, in with the new: Do a quick sweep of the fridge and get rid of anything that's rotting, outdated, and unrecognizable. As food prep becomes a regular part of your routine, you'll have much less waste and may be able to skip this first step altogether.

Wash, chop, and dance: When you put your groceries away, make a deal with yourself that you won't put anything in the produce bin until you've made it more edible in some way. If it's broccoli or cauliflower, wash and break it into florets. If it's carrots or celery, cut into snack-size pieces and submerge in water to keep them crisp and fresh. And why not put on some music and dance while you chop?

Recruit helpers: Families that prep together, stay together. So get your partner, kids, or housemates to join the fun. It will be chaotic at first, but once you find your rhythm it will go much faster and is a great way to interest the kids in healthy food. If you live alone, ask your friends or neighbors to participate in a weekly food prep get together.

Make it manageable: Establishing a sustainable food prep routine requires you to be realistic about your time and how you want to spend it. Unless you *love* to be in the kitchen and spend your spare time there, don't plan on making ten different recipes.

Set a timer—you can do anything for twenty minutes: This is an old trick for home organizing that works beautifully for food prep. Once you get home with the groceries, set a timer for twenty minutes and see how much you can get done. Tell yourself that whatever you get done is enough.

FOOD PREP CHECKLIST AND STORAGE TIPS

This checklist is similar to the one I use when I come home from the grocery store on Sunday mornings. I've prioritized it based on what will give you the most bang for your buck, starting with simpler tasks and adding on as you get more efficient with your food prep routine. You can pick, choose, and alter this list to suit your needs.

The bare essentials

☐ Wash all produce (fruit and vegetables).

☐ Chop veggies for salads and/or snacks.

☐ Store produce in green bags or glass containers (see storage tips).

Second-tier prep: All of the above plus . . .

☐ Make a big salad to be used as a side dish or lunch entrée.

☐ Cook quinoa, brown rice, or other whole grain (1 cup dry = 3 cups cooked).

☐ Make a pot of beans or cook up some lentils.

☐ Marinate and bake some tofu.

Third-tier prep: All of the above plus . . .

☐ Choose one or two recipes to make that you'd like to eat throughout the week.

Storage tips:

- Use a salad spinner to dry lettuce, then wrap it in paper towels and store in the crisper (no bag necessary). If you're using kale or chard, spin it off, and just put the lid on the spinner and store it in the refrigerator for four to five days.

- Store carrots, celery, jicama, and radishes in an airtight container full of water to keep them nice and crisp.

- Store fresh herbs in a small vase or glass that is half full of water (like a little bouquet!).

- Slice wet vegetables (e.g., cucumbers, peppers) on demand instead of chopping in advance.

- Use Debbie Meyer GreenBags or Bluapple to extend the life of your produce. Both control the ethylene that fruit and vegetables release, which accelerates ripening and ultimately leads to the early demise of your precious fruits and veggies.

- Use glass storage containers or mason jars to store leftovers and to freeze individual portions from large-batch recipes.

When to Eat Cake

Be Pro-Choice When It Comes to Food

One surefire way to feel like you're in an endless state of deprivation is to constantly tell yourself and others that you *can't* have something. Your new relationship with food is all about choosing with intention and being very deliberate about what you choose. You may decide that you're not going to partake in the all-you-can-eat ice cream sundae bar at your kid's best friend's birthday, but it's not because you *can't* have ice cream or chocolate fudge syrup or candy toppings. It's because you *choose* not to. It's that simple. You may need to remind yourself why you're choosing not to, like maybe the digestive consequences will be unbearable, or maybe it's because you don't really like ice cream sundaes to begin with and you're done gorging on foods you don't like just to be polite. Whatever it is, you're justified in your choice, and you don't need to explain to anyone. Except maybe yourself.

The flip side of this is, of course, is choosing to partake. And this is every bit as critical. You have to know when it's time to simply say, "Screw it! I want cake." So then you eat that cake with complete awareness. You engage all your senses, just like you've been practicing, and savor that cake like it's the best thing you're ever going to eat. Then comes the hard part. *Reject the guilt.* You know it's coming because that station has been programed in for decades. If you start to play the reel in your head that starts with "I shouldn't have . . . ," you can just say, "No, thank you. I'm not accepting any guilt today. I simply don't have room for it."

The other nuance of being "pro-choice" is that you also get to choose not to spiral out of control if you do decide to indulge. You no longer have to throw up your arms in defeat, feeling like you've blown the whole weekend, so you might as well keep punishing your body. You're done with that. You choose with intention, savor and enjoy, reject the guilt, then go right back to being that person who has a healthy relationship with food and your body. *That* is the decision that you get to make. Again, you get to choose.

Repeat after Me: I Will Not Fall into Another Dieting Trap

Remember that the dieting industry is a multibillion-dollar industry that can survive only if you keep doubting that you know how to eat. If every person became a mindful, intentional eater, stopped eating processed foods, and started eating a lot more plant-based foods, the dieting industry would go bankrupt. Unfortunately, that's not likely to happen anytime soon, so you'll have to deliberately tune out ads with svelte, sexy models trying to sell you the magic diet of the moment. You'll have to smile and nod when your well-meaning friends or family members tell you they're on the new starve-yourself-silly diet and have lost twenty pounds! Or better yet, hand them this book and tell them to read The Science of Eating versus the Art of Eating (page 7). Now that *you* know better, you can be an ambassador for change. If that's too ambitious for you, not to worry; just keep your head in the game and relish the fact that you've discovered an easier way where you don't have to be constantly at odds with your body.

Mastering Mindful Eating under Every Circumstance

DINING OUT

Restaurant dining presents a few unique challenges that can easily be overcome by preserving the mindful eating sensibilities you use at home.

- **Research the restaurant.** Look at the menu online and scope out the healthier options.

- **Take a pass on mindless grazing.** Just say no to the bread basket and bottomless bowl of tortilla chips.

- **Share food with your dining partner(s).** Enjoy the interaction.

- **Be selective about your indulgences.** Instead of having the "anything goes" attitude, choose between appetizers, wine, or dessert.

- **Eat like a food critic.** Enjoy small portions with a discerning palate.

- **Eat slowly.** Practice setting down your fork between bites. Be mindful of the flavors and textures and savor the food experience.

- **Ask the server to take your plate as soon as you feel satisfied.** That way, you're not tempted to keep nibbling until you're uncomfortably full.

- **Take a walk after your meal.** Check out the neighborhood, and make sure to park a few blocks away from the restaurant.

EATING WITH OTHERS

Eating in community is a beautiful thing and can also be done mindfully with just a little more awareness and attention.

- **Turn off the TV** and keep the cell phones away from the table.
- **Start with gratitude.** Open the meal by sharing what you're grateful for.
- **Dish up with intention.** Try taking a little less than what you think you need (remind yourself you can get more if you're still hungry).
- **Notice the food on your plate** and have the awareness that food is what brings you together.
- **Put the fork down between each bite** and strive to be the slowest eater at the table.
- **Give thanks** (silently or aloud) when you finish the meal.

HOLIDAY EATING

With family traditions and celebrations, holiday times provide a plethora of opportunities to practice your mindful eating skills. This is often a time when you become acutely aware of how family dynamics influence your eating behaviors. Remember that you have a right to make food choices that feel congruent with your new mindset, *especially* during times of celebration. Don't be afraid to redefine how you'd like to engage with food, family members, and friends on holidays and special gatherings.

- **Create new traditions** that are in keeping with your wellness vision.
- **Check in with your body** and honor the desire for nourishing foods, rest, and movement.
- **Prepare your feast** with family and friends and share the responsibility of cooking, serving, and cleaning up.
- **Volunteer as a family** to make or serve food to those who are less fortunate.

TRAVELING

STICK TO A ROUTINE: Get moving! Check to see if your hotel has a gym, or if there are nice walking paths in the city you are visiting. Try to not let travel derail your exercise routine—it may even help with travel stress!

PACK SNACKS: Easy-to-pack snacks can be a lifesaver when traveling. Whether you're on the plane or in between meetings, having balanced snack options at hand can help curb cravings by the end of a busy day. When possible, try pairing with something fresh, like a piece of fruit or vegetable sticks.

STAY HYDRATED: Flying and travel stress can dehydrate the body.

PREPARE AND PLAN

RESTAURANT SELECTIONS: If you have meetings scheduled during mealtimes, take a peek at the menu ahead of time so you feel prepared to make healthy choices.

HOTEL LOCATION: Scope out the location of your hotel. Consider the location of nearby grocery stores and in-room amenities such as a mini fridge or kitchenette.

BREAKFAST: You may likely eat most meals out, but can you bring anything along to ensure you have breakfast options each day? Oatmeal packets, granola, yogurt, and fruit may be easy options to have in your room.

CHECK IN WITH YOUR MENTAL HEALTH

Travel stress, missing partners and family, and even loneliness can affect your health on the road. Many people expense food or drinks to make traveling feel a bit more comforting. Explore nonfood rewards, such as a bath, to help unwind at the end of a long day.

Putting It All Together

Congratulations! If you've made it to this point in the book you've undoubtedly done some serious self-reflection. Perhaps you've had important insights into your eating behaviors and your mindset around food. Maybe you felt outraged about all of the confusion created by the dieting industry and our media culture. Hopefully you were able to relate to some of the stories that were shared throughout the book. But mostly I'm hoping that you have recognized that there's a more productive way to interact with food and honor your body wisdom and that you do not want to waste one more minute buying into the deception and being mad at your body.

Putting these concepts into practice takes time and requires patience. Keep reminding yourself that you're reprogramming some deep-seated beliefs about dieting and you're changing behaviors you've been engaging in for years or maybe even a lifetime. You *will* get triggered and sometimes fall back into old patterns, and that's perfectly okay. The most important part is that you observe those tendencies without judgment and course correct as soon as possible. Avoid falling into the trap of dwelling on perceived failures and defining yourself as someone who will never be a mindful eater. You were born with this ability. It belongs to you and you can claim it whenever you choose.

It's also important to identify ways in which you can feel supported in this journey and reach out for help and guidance when you need it. For some, making intentions known to family and friends can be enough to find the support and accountability that's needed. Others might benefit from assistance from trained professionals. Many of my patients have carefully assembled a care team that's just right for them, including a dietitian, therapist, naturopath, energy healer or meditation coach, hypnotherapist, and so on. For additional resources that you might find helpful, see page 190.

Recipes to Engage Your Senses

PART II

I t's time to play with your food! Every single time you eat it's an opportunity to have a complete sensory experience that brings pleasure, joy, and deep satisfaction into every meal. This is your chance to give food the respect it deserves and slow down enough to let your brain and your body know that you've been fed. These delicious recipes were designed to sharpen your senses and practice a whole new way of being with your food. You'll notice callout boxes on many of the recipes that encourage you to be aware of what you see, taste, smell, feel, and hear.

I describe this way of eating as a mini meditation, where you can unplug from the craziness of the day and be completely present for these sacred acts of self-nourishment. Don't worry if you don't consider yourself a master meditator—in fact, that's the best candidate for mindful eating! When your mind starts to wander and you start planning your day or thinking about all the things you need to do after you finish eating, simply bring your awareness back to your placemat. Notice the colors, textures, and aromas of your food. Pay attention to how your body is experiencing the food, noticing any sensations that arise. Put your fork down between bites, close your eyes, and really taste your food. You have full permission to make yummy noises while you eat. Start and finish each meal with gratitude for all of the abundance on your table and in your life.

All of the recipes featured here are plant based. You don't have to be a vegan, vegetarian, raw foodist, or anything else to be a mindful eater. I just happen to think that plant-based foods are nature's gift to us and they're perfectly poised to teach us a lesson in being satisfied with simple pleasures. That said, sometimes veggies just need to be dressed up a little to showcase their true essence, so I've taken the liberty to amp up the awesomeness.

Food as Art

F ood provides the perfect palate of color, texture, shape, and form to summon the artist within you. Allow yourself to be the graphic designer of your plate as you create edible works of art that stimulate your appetite and make you pause with reverence at the feast you have crafted with nature's offerings. We eat first with our eyes, so always take time to notice and appreciate how your food *looks* before ever lifting your fork.

Farmers' Market Grilled Pizza

Pizza doesn't have to be a delivery system for processed meat and cheese. It can be an artful showcase of garden-fresh vegetables, fruit, and herbs. I'll never forget making a thin-crust, grilled-veggie pizza for my eight-year-old niece who innocently asked, "What is that?" I proudly boasted that it was a pizza, of course! To which she replied, "No, Auntie M, that's a salad on a cracker." Be that as it may, we had a blast selecting seasonal ingredients at the market and assembling this creative variation of the meat-lover's pizza, and every last bite got eaten.

MAKES 4 SERVINGS

1 cup tightly packed fresh basil

2 tablespoons pine nuts

1 clove garlic

¼ cup extra-virgin olive oil, divided

2 teaspoons nutritional yeast

1½ teaspoons sea salt, divided

2 medium shallots, minced

6 shiitake mushrooms, sliced

2 medium red bell peppers, sliced

1 cup chopped broccoli, or 1 cup stemmed and chopped kale or chard

1 Japanese eggplant, sliced diagonally into ½-inch-thick ovals

2 teaspoons avocado oil

1 premade 9-inch pizza crust (frozen cauliflower crust or any crust of your choosing)

½ cup sliced artichoke hearts

1 teaspoon red pepper flakes

Preheat the grill to medium high (temperature about 350 degrees F).

To make the pesto, in a food processor or blender, blend the basil, pine nuts, garlic, 3 tablespoons of the olive oil, nutritional yeast, and ½ teaspoon of the salt until smooth. Add water if necessary.

In a large skillet over medium heat, heat the remaining 1 tablespoon olive oil and add the shallots. Sauté for about 3 minutes, until the shallots start to caramelize. Add the mushrooms and remaining 1 teaspoon salt and sauté for another 3 minutes, until mushrooms begin to get juicy. Add the peppers and broccoli, cover, and allow to steam for 3 to 4 minutes, stirring occasionally.

(CONTINUED)

Baste both sides of the eggplant with avocado oil and sprinkle with salt. Lay the eggplant out on the preheated grill. Cook for 4 to 5 minutes on each side, until eggplant starts to soften and brown. Remove from the grill and set aside. Place the crust on the grill and cook until the crust starts to brown (3 to 4 minutes on each side).

Assemble the pizza. Spread the pesto evenly over the crust. Add a layer of grilled eggplant and spread the sautéed veggies over the top. Evenly place the artichoke hearts on the pizza. Sprinkle with the red pepper flakes. Cut into 8 slices.

Rainbow Breakfast Bowl

Fruit provides such a colorful palate from which to create the most beautiful dishes. This is a summertime favorite for me, and it makes me so happy to start the day looking into a bowl that features all the colors of the rainbow. You can definitely swap out or add other vibrant types of fruit like golden kiwi, huckleberries, acai berries, dragon fruit (which is a stunning magenta color!), or any other fruit that catches your attention. You don't have to be an artist to make this look like a work of art.

Once you've arranged your bowl to your satisfaction, sit with your bowl in front of you and take a few moments to marvel at what nature provides. Notice the contrast in colors and textures. Do you start to salivate in anticipation of the bright and juicy mango?

MAKES 1 SERVING

½ cup plain coconut or soy yogurt

1 teaspoon honey

1 green kiwifruit, peeled and cut into rounds

1 Ataulfo mango (also known as honey or champagne mango), peeled and cut into chunks

½ cup fresh or frozen and thawed raspberries or strawberries

½ cup fresh or frozen and thawed blueberries

2 tablespoons coarsely chopped walnuts

1 tablespoon hemp hearts

1 tablespoon ground flaxseeds

Scoop the yogurt into the center of a cereal bowl. Artfully drizzle the honey over the yogurt. Arrange the kiwifruit in the center of the bowl. Make a circle around the kiwi with the mango, then add a row of raspberries and make a final border around the raspberries with the blueberries. Sprinkle the walnuts, hemp hearts, and flaxseed over the yogurt.

PRO TIP: You can also use 12-ounce mason jars and make these parfait style by stacking the fruit in layers with yogurt in between. This is a fun family project on Sundays to prep breakfast for part of the week.

Roasted Romanesco with Cannellini Beans and Black Rice

Romanesco is perhaps one of nature's most perfect forms of vegetable art. Its chartreuse color sets it apart from any other veg, and the textures and patterns are a sight to behold. Math nerds might appreciate that it's described as an approximate fractal pattern—I just like it because it looks kind of dangerous. If you're ever hoping to strike up a conversation in the produce section, pick up a head of Romanesco and confidently put it in your cart. People have lots of questions—can you really eat that? How do you prepare it? What does it taste like? I tell them it's like broccoli and cauliflower had a rebellious love child. Roasted Romanesco is a treat anytime, but the sharp contrast with the black rice and white beans in this dish is nothing less than stunning.

As your garlic is roasting and you're prepping the Romanesco, take a moment to really examine it. Notice how the spiky spirals organize themselves into a cone-like pattern. As you break it into the florets, take note of the beauty of each individual set of spirals—so many patterns and so much texture to take in with your eyes and feel with your fingertips.

MAKES 4 SERVINGS

1 head garlic

2 tablespoons extra-virgin olive oil, divided

1 cup Chinese black rice (e.g., Lotus Foods Forbidden Rice)

1¾ cups vegetable broth

1½ teaspoons sea salt, divided

1 head Romanesco, broken into florets

½ teaspoon freshly ground black pepper

1 (15-ounce) can cannellini beans or other small white beans

1 lemon (preferably Meyer lemon)

¼ cup chopped fresh basil

2 tablespoons fresh oregano

(CONTINUED)

Preheat the oven to 375 degrees F.

Slice the top off the head of garlic to expose the cloves. Drizzle with 1 teaspoon of the oil and wrap the head in aluminum foil. Place in the oven and roast for 45 to 50 minutes. You're giving the garlic a head start. The Romanesco will join the party in progress.

Meanwhile, in a medium saucepan or stockpot over high heat, put the rice, broth, and ½ teaspoon salt and bring to a boil. Reduce heat, cover, and simmer for 30 to 35 minutes, until all liquid is absorbed.

In a large bowl, toss the Romanesco with 2 teaspoons of the oil. Sprinkle with ½ teaspoon of the salt and the pepper. Spread on a baking sheet and place in the preheated oven with the garlic for 15 to 20 minutes. Remove the Romanesco and garlic from oven and transfer the Romanesco to a large bowl. Add the rice and beans.

Pour the remaining 1 tablespoon oil into a small bowl. Squeeze in 2 to 3 cloves of the roasted garlic (wrap the rest to save and use later). Use a fork to mash the garlic. Add ½ teaspoon zest from the lemon then cut the lemon in half and add 1 tablespoon lemon juice. Stir in the basil, oregano, and remaining ½ teaspoon salt. Add to the Romanesco, beans, and rice and toss until well coated.

Cast-Iron Beets and Sweets Medley

A cast-iron skillet is your palette for this lovely creation, and when you bring the skillet to the table to serve your guests, the oohs and aahs will be audible. It's a beautiful dish that's fun to put together. If you have a mandoline, it's easier to get a precise slice on the beets and yams, but don't let it deter if you have to hand slice them. In either case, you have a lovely, colorful array of rounds to decoratively arrange around the perimeter of the pan like the petals of a flower, with the cauliflower florets resting playfully in the center. This dish has a rustic charm, and it tastes great too. In fact, this is the perfect dish to get beet bad-mouths on board.

MAKES 6 SERVINGS

1 tablespoon plus 2 teaspoons
   extra-virgin olive oil
4 medium crimson beets, skin on,
   greens removed
1 large garnet yam, peeled
1 head garlic

1 small head cauliflower,
   separated into florets
1 teaspoon sea salt
1 teaspoon nutritional yeast
3 rosemary sprigs
2 teaspoons fresh thyme

Preheat the oven to 350 degrees F.

Use the 2 teaspoons olive oil to grease a 9-inch cast-iron skillet.

Slice the beets into ⅛-inch-thick rounds and the yam into ¼-inch-thick rounds. Separate and peel the garlic cloves. Alternate the beets and yams around the inner edge of the skillet, so that they're leaning against the edge and slightly overlapping. Wedge garlic cloves between some of the rounds.

(CONTINUED)

Place the cauliflower in the middle of the skillet. Drizzle the 1 tablespoon oil over the veggies. Sprinkle with the salt and nutritional yeast. Cover with aluminum foil and bake for 30 minutes. Remove from oven and take off the aluminum foil.

Arrange the rosemary sprigs around the skillet and add the thyme, spreading evenly over the veggies. Return to oven and bake for another 30 minutes uncovered, until the cauliflower begins to turn golden brown. Serve in the skillet.

PRO TIP: If you're a beet lover, you can go all in with golden beets in place of the yams. The overall flavor is a little bit earthier and less sweet. You can also add onion rings (meaning onions cut into rounds, not the deep-fried rings) for another dimension of flavor.

Beauty Bowls

Bowls of all sorts have become trendy in the wellness world, and for good reason. If you suffer from salad fatigue, or you just want to feel like you're eating something different, try channeling your inner artist by arranging your bowl ingredients in a way that delights you. I go for color first, flavor second, texture third. The point is, there's no wrong way to assemble ingredients for your bowl. You have complete permission to play with your food and do what makes you happy!

Winning combinations:

· Quinoa, black beans, steamed or roasted broccolini, red peppers, salsa, sliced avocado

· Riced cauliflower, lentils, stewed tomatoes, spinach, curry sauce

· Farro, white beans, baby kale, sun-dried tomatoes, vegan pesto

MAKES 1 SERVING

For the base
½ cup cooked whole grain or starchy veggie (e.g., roasted yams, new potatoes, or squash)
½ cup canned beans or lentils
1 cup greens (e.g., spinach, chard, kale, baby kale, mixed greens)
½ cup red/purple veggies (e.g., purple cabbage, sliced red bell peppers, tomatoes, crimson beets)
½ cup other veggies (e.g., carrots, cauliflower, broccoli, roasted brussels sprouts)

Dressing options
2 tablespoons dressing (e.g., vinaigrette, pesto, salsa, guacamole, garlic sauce, tahini)

Topping options
Nuts, sunflower seeds, pumpkin seeds, sesame seeds, fresh or dried herbs

In a medium bowl, artfully arrange all ingredients.

Hands-on Foods

Connecting with your food as it's plucked from the earth, pulled from a tree, or harvested from the vine reminds you where your food came from. Using your own two hands to process the food for cooking—massaging, rolling, kneading, and chopping—creates a harmonious energy exchange between you and the food. All too often utensils become the barrier to enjoying the tactile experience of bringing nourishment to your body, hand to mouth. Leave the flatware in the drawer and feel the weight, texture, and temperature of the food. Let your fingertips preview your culinary delights.

Basil Mint Fresh Rolls

I like to have all hands on deck when I make fresh rolls. It's such an interactive food experience and it's the perfect opportunity to get others involved in the fun. Prepping the veggies for fresh roll assembly is the most time-consuming part, so it's good to have a few friends with knife skills to pitch in. When it comes to assembly, place all the veggies in separate bowls and set them up so they're within easy reach of the rice wrappers. Take turns loading up the rice wrappers with the beautiful array of veggies and herbs and neatly rolling them. It takes a few tries to get a feel for how to build the perfect roll, but once you get the hang of it, you'll see each roll as a little work of art.

Notice the texture of the rice wrappers before placing them in water and feel with your fingertips how the texture changes as the rice paper softens in the water. Make contact with all the ingredients as you place them in the wrapper and pay attention to the whole sensory experience as you're rolling, dipping, and eating the delicious fresh rolls you created with your own two hands.

MAKES 6 SERVINGS

½ teaspoon sea salt

1 package glass noodles

2 medium carrots, shredded

2 English cucumbers, thinly sliced

1 large red bell pepper, thinly sliced

1 cup sprouts or microgreens

1 bunch fresh basil

1 bunch fresh mint

1 package 9-inch round rice wrappers

In a medium saucepan, heat 3 cups water and salt over high heat. Bring to a boil and add the noodles. Cook the glass noodles for 1 minute, then drain and rinse the noodles.

Put all the herbs and veggies in small bowls for easy access.

(CONTINUED)

Add warm water to a pie pan until it is about half full. Place individual rice wrappers in the water and soak until soft (about 1 minute). Remove the rice wrapper from water and place on a tea towel.

Place a small pile of the carrots, cucumbers, peppers, and sprouts in the center of the rice wrapper, roll one edge over the veggies, and place a whole basil leaf and 2 to 3 mint leaves on top of the edge that is rolled over the veggies. Fold the edges in and continue to roll like a burrito. You should be able to see the basil and mint leaves through the thin layers of the rice wrapper. Slice each roll in half and artfully display them on a platter with dipping sauces in the center of the platter or stationed nearby.

PRO TIP: Fresh rolls will stay good in the refrigerator for at least 3 days and they pack well, so they're perfect to take for lunch or a fancy afternoon snack.

Peanut Dipping Sauce

3 tablespoons chunky peanut butter
1 teaspoon peeled, minced ginger
1 clove garlic, minced
⅓ cup vegetable broth

3 tablespoons tamari sauce
  (or coconut aminos)
2 tablespoons rice vinegar
2 teaspoons agave nectar

In a small mixing bowl, combine all ingredients and whisk until smooth.

Soy-Ginger Dipping Sauce

½ cup freshly squeezed lime juice (from
  3 to 4 medium limes)
⅓ cup tamari sauce (or coconut aminos)
¼ cup water

2 tablespoons agave nectar
1 clove garlic, minced
1 teaspoon peeled, minced ginger

In a small mixing bowl, combine all ingredients and whisk until smooth.

Sexy, Smoky Jackfruit Tostadas

Jackfruit is a sensuous, mysterious fruit. It has a green, prickly outer shell that makes you wonder how anyone ever discovered the luscious fruit that lives inside. The immature fruit has a neutral flavor but has the magical ability to emulate the texture of pulled pork when it's cooked *and* it will take on the flavor of whatever spices you cook it with. When the fruit ripens and matures, it sweetens up and tastes more like a cross between a pineapple and a banana. Jackfruit enthusiasts have made it easy for us to eat the young jackfruit by selling it in a can or in refrigerated pouches (where the jackfruit is often already marinated in a savory or spicy sauce).

MAKES 6 SERVINGS

2 (20-ounce) cans green jackfruit

2 teaspoons avocado oil

1 small white or yellow onion, chopped

1 small garnet yam, peeled and cut into ½-inch cubes

3 cloves garlic, minced

1 (4.5-ounce) can diced green chiles

½ cup sliced fire-roasted peppers (frozen or marinated in a jar)

1 tablespoon freshly squeezed lime juice

1 tablespoon chipotle chili powder

⅛ teaspoon cayenne (more if you want to turn up the heat)

½ teaspoon sea salt

6 corn tortillas

1 (15-ounce) can vegan refried beans (I prefer the refried black beans)

1 large avocado, pitted and chopped into chunks

2 cups shredded cabbage (purple or green—or a combo of both!)

Drain and rinse the jackfruit. Cut the triangular pieces into smaller strips or pull them apart with your hands for a more tactile experience. It should start to take on the appearance of shredded meat.

(CONTINUED)

In a large skillet or Dutch oven over medium heat, heat the avocado oil. Add the onion and sauté for about 3 minutes, until the onions start to soften. Add the cubed yams. Cover and let steam for 5 minutes, stirring occasionally. Add the jackfruit, garlic, chiles with liquid from the can, roasted peppers, lime juice, chili powder, cayenne, and salt. Reduce heat to medium low, cover, and let simmer for another 10 to 15 minutes, stirring frequently.

While the jackfruit mixture is simmering, set the oven on broil—high heat. Spread the tortillas out on a bare baking sheet. Place in the oven and flip the tortillas every couple of minutes until they start to brown and become crisp. This takes about 6 minutes, but watch them carefully because they can burn easily under the broiler.

Assemble the tostadas with the tortilla as the first layer, followed by the refried beans, the jackfruit mixture, avocado, and cabbage.

Mediterranean Snack Platter

This is my sneaky way of offering a healthier version of the usual meat, cheese, and cracker tray. It's gluten- and dairy-free, but no one ever notices that because they're immediately drawn in by the colorful peppers, the creamy hummus, the salty-fatty olives, and the crunchy almonds (I use Marcona almonds seasoned with rosemary or truffle salt). Challenge yourself to expand the ingredient list with some of your Mediterranean favorites. Pay attention to texture, color, and flavor combos. I often add marinated artichoke hearts or mushrooms, cherry tomatoes, and sometimes smoked salmon. You can swap out the hummus with baba ganoush (eggplant dip) or offer tapenade instead of mixed olives. The possibilities are endless!

MAKES 6 SERVINGS

1 cup hummus (can be store-bought or use the recipe that follows)

1 cup mixed olives (e.g., kalamata, Castelvetrano, Spanish green olives)

1 cup marinated artichoke hearts

1 large red bell pepper, sliced

1 large yellow bell pepper, sliced

1 English cucumber, cut into spears

½ cup Marcona almonds

Place the hummus in a dish in the center of a large platter. Arrange the olives, artichoke hearts, and veggies around the dish of hummus. Sprinkle the almonds around the outer edge of the platter. Have fun decorating this platter in a way that looks visually appealing to you!

Basic Hummus

1 (15-ounce) can chickpeas, drained and
  rinsed
2 cloves garlic
1 tablespoon tahini

3 tablespoons extra-virgin olive oil
1 tablespoon freshly squeezed lemon
  juice
1 teaspoon sea salt

Put all ingredients in a food processor or blender and blend until smooth. Add water if you like a creamier, smoother texture.

Moroccan Chickpea Burgers

Veggie burgers can be tricky. Sometimes they get crumbly and don't hold up well during frying or grilling, but these chickpea burgers are an exception. The ingredients bind well, and the flavors are spectacular, so you won't miss the meat. It may sound strange to put cinnamon and nutmeg into a savory chickpea patty, but the flavor combo really works, and the sweeter spices play exceptionally well with the umami flavors. You can put these bad boys on regular buns, gluten-free buns, or brioche rolls, or wrap them in large lettuce leaves. You can also purchase mini buns and convert them into sliders to serve at parties. Your vegan guests will be delighted!

There's nothing quite like the tactile experience of eating a burger on a bun. Notice the weight and height of the burger as you hold it with both hands. Feel yourself salivate as you anticipate the first bite. Notice how the texture changes as your teeth sink through the bun, the toppings, and the chickpea patty.

MAKES 4 SERVINGS

2 tablespoons avocado oil, divided
1 small yellow onion, diced
8 shiitake mushrooms, sliced
1 teaspoon sea salt, divided
2 cloves garlic, minced
3 medium carrots, shredded
1 (15-ounce) can chickpeas, drained

2 teaspoons ground cumin
1 teaspoon minced peeled ginger
1 teaspoon sweet paprika
¾ teaspoon ground cinnamon
½ teaspoon ground nutmeg
¼ cup gluten-free all-purpose flour

In a large skillet over medium heat, heat 2 teaspoons of the avocado oil. Add the onions and sauté for about 3 minutes, until they start to soften. Add the mushrooms and ½ teaspoon salt and sauté for another 2 minutes. Mix in the garlic and carrots and sauté for another 3 to 4 minutes, stirring occasionally. Transfer the mixture to a food processor or blender.

(CONTINUED)

Add the chickpeas, remaining ½ teaspoon salt, and the cumin, ginger, paprika, cinnamon, and nutmeg to the food processor and pulse a few times until combined but still chunky. Transfer the mixture to a large mixing bowl and stir in the flour. Form the mixture into 4 patties, approximately ¾ inch thick. Refrigerate the patties for at least 20 minutes.

Clean and dry the large skillet, and place over medium-high heat. Heat the remaining 1 tablespoon plus 1 teaspoon of oil. Place the patties in the skillet and fry for 3 to 4 minutes per side until the patties begin to brown and crisp. Remove from heat and transfer to your favorite gluten-free bun or use a lettuce wrap.

Five-Spice Tofu Sushi Rolls

Not a raw fish enthusiast? Don't let that stop you from enjoying the sushi experience. Well-seasoned tofu works nicely in this creative combo of ingredients. Chinese black rice (also known as forbidden rice) adds interest (and nutrients!) to this nontraditional sushi roll. Invite some friends to lend their hands because the preparation is half the fun. I've been known to host sushi-rolling parties that inevitably evolve into a sake-fueled, friendly competition to see who can create the superior sushi roll.

Bamboo sushi rolling mats can be useful when perfecting your rolling technique. They also add to the sensory experience. If you don't have bamboo mats, there's no need to fret. Tea towels can also be used to aid in rolling.

MAKES 6 ROLLS

2 tablespoons coconut oil

1 tablespoon tamari

2 teaspoons five-spice powder (blend of cinnamon, clove, fennel, star anise, and white pepper)

½ teaspoon minced peeled ginger

8 ounces extra-firm tofu (Wildwood's High-Protein Tofu works well)

1 cup Chinese black rice (e.g., Lotus Foods Forbidden Rice)

2 cups mushroom broth

6 nori sheets

3 medium carrots, julienned

2 large daikon radishes, julienned

2 tablespoons sesame seeds

Wasabi and tamari, for dipping (optional)

Preheat the oven to 400 degrees F.

In a small cast-iron skillet over medium heat, melt the coconut oil. Add the tamari, five-spice, and ginger. Stir until well combined and turn off heat.

Wrap the tofu in paper towels and very gently squeeze out some of the excess water. The high-protein tofu is dense and does not have a lot of excess water. Slice the tofu into 3-by-1-inch strips that are about ½ inch thick. Place the strips in the cast-iron skillet so the bottom gets coated in the sauce. Then flip each strip and place the skillet in the oven. Bake for 30 minutes, flipping the tofu after 15 minutes. Tofu should start to brown and look slightly crispy around the edges.

In a large saucepan over medium-high heat, heat the rice and broth and bring to a boil. Reduce the heat to medium low, cover, and simmer for about 25 minutes, until all liquid is absorbed. This can also be done in an Instant Pot, just reduce the broth by ¼ cup and set manual pressure cooker for 12 minutes. Allow to depressurize naturally.

Lay out the nori sheets (spritz with water for easy rolling). Place one strip of tofu on a nori sheet. Top with about 3 tablespoons of rice, 4 to 5 carrot slices, 3 to 4 daikon slices, and a pinch of sesame seeds. Carefully roll the nori sheet like a burrito, folding the ends in as you go. Repeat until you run out of ingredients. If you want it to look more sushi-like, you can leave the ends of the roll open, but it will be messier to eat. If using, combine the wasabi and tamari in a small bowl and use as a dipping sauce.

> PRO TIP: You can double the amount of tofu you bake and use the leftover rice and veggies to assemble deconstructed sushi bowls that are perfect to pack for lunch.

Pop, Sizzle, Crunch

If we listen carefully enough, we hear a symphony of kitchen sounds every time we prepare food; the rhythm of chopping, the beat of a wooden spoon rapping against the skillet, the sizzling and popping of hot oil, the whirring and buzzing of blenders and hand mixers. You're the maestro and musician of the orchestra in your kitchen. If Act 1 in your musical is food preparation, Act 2 is the tempo of eating; the crunch of the carrots in the salad, the sipping of the soup from the spoon, the audible yummy noises that escape from your mouth in appreciation of the tasty creations. Cleanup is the final act, with the melody of silverware clanking and dishes being stacked, and the soothing rush of the water as it clears the waste away. Appreciate every sound and find more joy in cooking, eating, and yes, even cleanup.

Easy Cheezy Popped Sorghum

This itty, bitty popcorn look-alike is crazy cute! I don't know what it is about miniature food that entices me, but I love to discover smaller versions of well-known foods. Sorghum is a nutritious, gluten-free grain that looks a little like millet. It's a nice alternative for those who are sensitive to corn and are really missing their popcorn on movie night. Sorghum is fun to pop, even though not all the grains will cooperate. Sprinkling nutritional yeast on this popped grain reminds me of the shaker of Parmesan cheese from my youth, which I used liberally on many of the foods I ate. You'll love the salty/savory/tangy flavor!

MAKES 2 SERVINGS

1 tablespoon avocado oil

½ cup sorghum

1 tablespoon nutritional yeast

¼ teaspoon sea salt

In a large saucepan over medium-high heat, heat the avocado oil. Add the sorghum and swirl around in the pan until the grains are coated. Cover the pan and wait for that first exciting pop. Hold the lid in place and gently shake the pan over the burner every 20 to 30 seconds until most of the kernels pop (be prepared to have as many as half of those little devils not being cooperative enough to pop—but don't sacrifice the popped kernels by waiting too long because they'll start to burn).

Transfer the popped kernels to your favorite popcorn bowl and toss with the nutritional yeast and salt until well coated.

Crispy Beans and Seeds

Satisfying, healthy, crunchy snacks can be hard to come by. Crispy chickpeas paved the way, so why not try other combinations of beans and seeds? Start with cannellini beans and pinto beans as recommended in this recipe, then have fun playing with any and all of your favorite legumes (baby limas, fava, flageolet, navy beans, edamame—you name it!).

MAKES 6 SERVINGS

1 tablespoon granulated garlic
2 teaspoons ground cumin
1 teaspoon ground coriander
2 teaspoons sea salt
¼ teaspoon cayenne
1 (15-ounce) can cannellini beans, drained and rinsed

1 (15-ounce) can pinto beans, drained and rinsed
1 tablespoon plus 2 teaspoons extra-virgin olive oil
1 cup raw, unsalted pepitas (shelled pumpkin seeds)
½ cup raw, unsalted sunflower seeds

Preheat the oven to 350 degrees F. Cover a baking sheet with parchment paper, or lightly grease it.

In a small bowl, combine the garlic, cumin, coriander, salt, and cayenne.

Pat the cannellini and pinto beans dry with a paper towel, then put in a medium bowl. Toss with the 1 tablespoon oil. Season with 1 tablespoon of the spice mixture and stir until the beans are well coated.

Spread the beans on the prepared baking sheet and bake for 40 minutes. While baking, put the pepitas and sunflower seeds in a small bowl. Toss with the 2 teaspoons oil, sprinkle with 2 teaspoons of the spice mixture, and stir until well coated. Add the seeds to the baking sheet with the beans after the beans have cooked for 40 minutes. Return to oven and bake for an additional 10 to 15 minutes, until seeds start to get crispy and are lightly browned.

Serve immediately or cool thoroughly before placing in an open-air container.

Lettuce-less Salad with Creamy Cilantro–Lime Dressing

This is a shout-out to all of my clients who have apologized for not liking salads because they don't care for lettuce. Well, forget the lettuce! Maybe that's an essential ingredient in a traditional salad, but it's not necessary for this fresh, crunchy, well-dressed masterpiece. I realize that cilantro is polarizing, so if you love cilantro, this will likely become your favorite dressing. If you hate cilantro, try using Italian parsley instead. You'll still that get that bright, clean tang that so elegantly complements the stronger flavors of the cauliflower and radishes.

MAKES 4 SERVINGS

For the base
1 cup snap peas
1 small head cauliflower,
    broken into large florets
12 radishes, quartered, or
    12 cherry tomatoes, halved
3 medium carrots, shredded
1 cup edamame, frozen and shelled

For the dressing
1 medium avocado, pitted and scooped
¼ cup chopped cilantro
1 tablespoon freshly squeezed lemon
    juice (preferably from Meyer lemon)
1 teaspoon honey
½ teaspoon sea salt
¼ teaspoon ground white pepper
½ cup water
¼ cup slivered almonds

Cut the snap peas on the bias. Hold the blade of your knife so that it's at an angle to the pea. Cut the pea into thirds, making sure to keep the blade angled so the resulting cut goes diagonally across the pea. Place in a large bowl.

Toss the cauliflower florets into a food processor and pulse several times until the cauliflower is broken down into small pieces. You can also do this with a knife if you don't have a food processor or just purchase riced cauliflower. Add the cauliflower to the bowl and toss in the radishes or tomatoes, carrots, and edamame.

To make the dressing, in a food processor or blender, put the avocado, cilantro, lemon juice, honey, salt, and pepper. Blend well and drizzle in the water until the dressing is the texture of a ranch dressing. Gradually add dressing to the bowl of veggies and toss until well coated. Add the slivered almonds and divide into four servings.

PRO TIP: You can double the dressing ingredients and use the leftovers as a dip for your cut veggies as an invigorating afternoon snack. The dressing keeps in the refrigerator for 4 to 5 days.

Root Veggie Fries with Smoky Tomato Dipping Sauce

Do you ever wonder what makes the sweet potato fries you get in restaurants crispier than the baked version you make at home? Well, part of the trick is to coat the fries with some type of flour and seasoning. Another trick is to deep-fry but you can still get some decent crispiness by just using a flour-and-spice coating. Especially if you hit them with the broiler toward the end of the bake time. Sweet potato fries are great, but try going outside of your comfort zone with root veggies you've never tried before. This is also a great way to get those finicky kiddos to eat a wider variety of veggies.

Be alert to the sounds around you as you produce these tasty gems. Notice how the knife sounds when it first pierces the skin of the veggies, then how it travels through the root, and finally lands on the cutting board in that definitive, satisfying way.

MAKES 4 SERVINGS

¼ cup gluten-free all-purpose flour

1 tablespoon nutritional yeast

1 teaspoon granulated garlic

1 teaspoon sea salt

1 large parsnip

2 medium carrots

1 large rutabaga, or 2 Yukon gold
  potatoes

1½ tablespoons avocado oil

1 tablespoon wheat-free tamari

For the dipping sauce

½ cup fire-roasted tomatoes

2 tablespoons tomato paste

1 tablespoon blackstrap molasses

2 teaspoons pure maple syrup

1 teaspoon smoked paprika

Preheat the oven to 425 degrees F. Line a baking sheet with parchment paper or lightly grease it.

In a small bowl, mix the flour, yeast, garlic, and salt.

(CONTINUED)

(CONTINUED)

Leave the peel on the parsnip, carrots, and rutabaga and cut into matchsticks (about the size of your finger). Transfer to a large bowl. Combine the avocado oil and tamari in a small bowl and drizzle over the veggies. Add the flour-and-spice mixture and toss until the veggies are well coated.

Spread the fries out on the prepared baking sheet. Bake until the fries begin to brown and crisp, 25 to 30 minutes. If you like a crispier fry, you can broil on high for just a couple of minutes until they're brown and crispy.

Meanwhile, to make the dipping sauce, blend the tomatoes, tomato paste, molasses, maple syrup, and paprika in a blender until smooth. Transfer to a small bowl for dipping.

Crimson Beets and Purple Cabbage Kraut

One of my favorite ways to incorporate more fermented foods into my diet is to add a generous scoop of kraut into my salad. It lends a satisfying crunch and tangy, acidic flavor that is similar to what vinegar brings to a dressing. You can manipulate the crunch factor by changing the shred size of the beets and cabbage—a thicker shred will lead to a crunchier kraut. Fermentation time also alters the texture, so if you want a crunchier kraut, a shorter fermentation time will work better for you. Watch and listen as your kraut comes to life over the days (or weeks, if you're patient enough). You might see and hear some bubbling as evidence of the lacto-fermentation. I imagine it as a progressive party going on in the jar. Every day more of those wild and crazy partygoers like *L. mesenteroides, L. plantarum,* and *L. brevis* show up to join the fun and pretty soon there's a raging party going on in my kitchen!

MAKES 2 QUARTS

1 (2-pound) head of purple cabbage
2 medium crimson beets

1½ tablespoons sea salt

Remove the outer leaves of the cabbage and reserve a large piece to cover the kraut. Shred the rest of the cabbage using the shredding attachment on a food processor or a mandoline. You can also shred with a knife if preferred. Transfer to a large bowl.

Peel and shred the beets and add to the bowl. Sprinkle in the salt and massage it into the cabbage and beets with your hands—yep! It's messy and will stain your hands a nice pink color that might last through the day.

(CONTINUED)

(CONTINUED)

Transfer the cabbage-and-beet mixture to a 2-quart jar, one handful at a time, pressing the mixture into the jar with your fist. Leave about 1.5 inches of head-space. Use the lid from the jar as a template to cut the reserved cabbage leaf into a circle to place on top of the kraut. Place a small jar filled with water on top of the leaf (baby food jars work great for this!). There should be a layer of brine sitting on top of the cabbage leaf.

Place the jar on a pie pan or plate and cover the jar with a tea towel. Tuck it away in a dark corner of your kitchen and allow to ferment for a minimum of 4 days. The longer you ferment, the more beneficial bacteria you get, and the tangier the kraut. I like to ferment for 10 to 14 days.

> PRO TIP: The great thing about fermentation is that it significantly increases the shelf life of your cabbage. Once you're done fermenting, close up the jar or transfer to smaller jars and move them to the refrigerator. They'll keep for a good 2 months (and probably longer!).

Aromatic
Pleasures

Sense of smell is a strong determinant for how we experience flavor. Even though taste and smell have different receptor organs, they are intimately connected by signals that go to the brain. Engage your olfactory system by using more herbs and spices. Your spice cabinet is the perfumery of your kitchen. Be a chemist of aromas and learn how to strike a balance of flavors by putting your nose to work. The nose knows how to entice the taste buds.

Slow-Cooked Cuban Black Beans

The best part about cooking anything in a slow cooker is that you come home at the end of the day and the whole house smells like a home-cooked meal. As soon as your mouth starts watering, dinner is served! No waiting necessary. These beans are delicious right out of the pot, and can be used as a side dish, main dish, or hearty snack. I love to pair this dish with roasted yams and charred broccoli. They're also great featured in a taco bar with shredded cabbage, rice, corn tortillas, and fresh guacamole.

MAKES 6 SERVINGS

1 cup dried black beans, soaked overnight

3 cups water

1 poblano pepper, seeded and diced

1 small yellow onion, diced

2 cloves garlic, minced

1 tablespoon dried oregano

2 teaspoons ground coriander

Zest from 1 lime

1 tablespoon apple cider vinegar

1 bay leaf

2 teaspoons sea salt

In a strainer, drain the black beans and rinse thoroughly. Put them in a slow cooker, then add the water, poblano, onion, garlic, oregano, coriander, zest, vinegar, and bay leaf. Cook on low for 4 to 6 hours. Remove the bay leaf and add salt ½ teaspoon at time, tasting after each addition.

These beans just keep getting better over the next few days! You can store in the refrigerator for up to 4 days and they will keep in the freezer for up to 6 months.

Pumpkin Pie Granola

Homemade granola of any sort fills your home with the mouthwatering smell of something akin to fresh-baked oatmeal cookies. I love that the aroma lingers for hours after the granola is cooled and put away. Now imagine all the divine scents of pumpkin pie joining in to create the ultimate olfactory sensation. Cinnamon, nutmeg, and cardamom are a trio of pure bliss that could be called the perfume of Thanksgiving. The deep, rich, and sweet earthiness of the roasted pecans absolutely seals the deal.

MAKES 6 SERVINGS

4 cups rolled oats

½ cup buckwheat groats

¼ cup maple syrup

2 tablespoons coconut palm sugar

1 tablespoon ground cinnamon

2 teaspoons ground nutmeg

2 teaspoons ground cardamom

¾ cup canned pumpkin

½ cup chopped pecans

Preheat the oven to 350 degrees F. In a large bowl, combine all ingredients except for the pecans and mix thoroughly. Spread mixture evenly onto a large baking sheet or 2 smaller baking sheets lined with parchment paper or lightly greased baking sheet. The granola should not be more than ¼ inch thick for best results. Bake for 30 minutes, stirring the mixture after 15 minutes and adding the pecans. Look for a golden-brown color and remove from the oven before it starts to turn a darker brown.

Allow the granola to cool completely before transferring to an airtight container.

Lentil Bolognese over Baked Yams

This meatless version of bolognese is so rich and hearty that your carnivorous friends won't even miss the meat. I love to slow cook this sauce in my Instant Pot on a rainy Sunday afternoon. And since the yams take a bit of time to cook, I think it's wise to bake a few extras and toss them in the freezer for another rainy day. The sauce will freeze well, too, and is so versatile! You can use it in the more traditional way, over pasta (or gluten-free pasta), or try it with zucchini or squash noodles. I can promise that it makes zucchini noodles a lot more interesting.

Take time to stop and smell the aromatics. While you're sautéing the mirepoix (onions, celery, and carrots) along with the garlic, close your eyes and breathe deeply through your nose. Before you add the wine, swirl it around a bit and see if you can pick out any hints of specific fruits or spices. When you're chopping the rosemary and basil, notice any salivary response you might have to the bright, fragrant smells of the fresh herbs.

MAKES 4 TO 6 SERVINGS

4 medium garnet yams
2 teaspoons extra-virgin olive oil
1 small yellow onion, diced
2 stalks celery, diced
1 large carrot, diced
3 cloves garlic, minced
1 (28-ounce) can diced tomatoes
1½ cups vegetable or mushroom broth

¼ cup dry red wine
½ cup dried red lentils
½ cup dried gray or black lentils
¼ cup fresh chopped basil
1 tablespoon dried Italian herbs
1 tablespoon fresh chopped rosemary
1 teaspoon sea salt

Preheat the oven to 400 degrees F.

Individually wrap the garnet yams in aluminum foil. Use a fork to poke several holes in each yam, piercing the aluminum foil and the skin of the yams. Place

(CONTINUED)

directly on the oven rack and bake for 50 to 60 minutes, until easy to pierce with a fork.

While yams are baking, heat the oil in a Dutch oven or stockpot over medium heat. Add the onions, celery, carrots, and garlic, and sauté until onions start to soften, about 5 minutes. Add the tomatoes, broth, and red wine.

Rinse the lentils in a fine strainer then add them to the pot along with the basil, Italian herbs, rosemary, and salt. Stir until ingredients are well combined. Cover and allow to simmer for 35 to 40 minutes, stirring occasionally.

PRO TIP: You can also make this bolognese sauce in a slow cooker—just put all ingredients in the slow cooker and simmer for 4 hours on low.

Toasted Pecan and Quinoa Fritters

There's something about the scent of sage that evokes a feeling of peacefulness and renewal for me. If I close my eyes and take a big whiff, I'm transported deep into the forest, surrounded by pine trees with the smell of the damp earth beneath me. When I'm using sage in a recipe, I know that the food that I'm making will be grounding and healing. This recipe features some of my most favored ingredients, all of which I keep stocked in my kitchen at all times. Serve these crispy fritters over a bed of arugula or any of your favorite greens, topped with a generous drizzle of Karam's Garlic Sauce (found in the refrigerated section of most grocery stores, near the hummus and dips).

Saging or "smudging" is an ancient practice, often used by indigenous peoples, to cleanse or clear a space. You can purchase a bundle of sage that is ideal for burning. The smoke from the burning sage is thought to be purifying. If you try this at home, be sure to hold a small plate beneath the burning sage. Or you can just settle for cooking with sage and allowing it to purify you from the inside out.

MAKES 12 SERVINGS

1 cup quinoa
½ cup dried black lentils
2¼ cups vegetable broth
1 cup pecans
1 teaspoon dried sage
1 teaspoon dried thyme
2 small carrots, grated

1 small zucchini, grated
½ cup sun-dried tomatoes packed in
    olive oil
½ teaspoon sea salt
¼ to ½ cup gluten-free all-purpose flour
1 tablespoon avocado oil

(CONTINUED)

Preheat the oven to 350 degrees F.

Rinse the quinoa and put it in a large saucepan. Add the lentils and vegetable broth and bring to a boil. Reduce heat to low, cover, and cook for 20 minutes until liquid is absorbed. Remove lid and fluff with a fork.

Spread the pecans on a baking sheet and place in the oven until lightly toasted, 5 to 7 minutes. Remove from oven and transfer to the food processor or to a cutting board if you want to hand chop. Finely chop the pecans while adding the sage and thyme. Set aside.

In a large bowl, combine 2 cups of the cooked quinoa-lentil mixture with the pecans. Add the carrots and zucchini. Chop the sun-dried tomatoes and add to the mixture. Sprinkle in the salt and mix until well combined. Add the flour until mixture holds together enough to form small patties.

In a large skillet over medium-high heat, heat the avocado oil. Drop the formed quinoa patties into the skillet and cook for about 2 minutes, then flip and cook for another 2 minutes until the patties are lightly browned and crispy. Remove from the pan and serve warm.

Savory Coconut–Lime Black Rice

I'm a fan of black rice. It's so much more exciting than brown rice, and who can resist eating "forbidden rice"? Jazzing it up with coconut milk, ginger, and lime leaves transforms a simple side dish into the star of the show. I know that lime leaves can be tricky to find in some areas, but they're certainly worth the hunt. You can substitute one tablespoon of lime zest, but it won't release that mouthwatering citrusy fragrance that lime leaves are notorious for.

MAKES 4 SERVINGS

1¼ cups vegetable broth
1 cup Chinese black rice (e.g., Lotus
    Foods Forbidden Rice)
½ cup unsweetened coconut milk

1 teaspoon fresh grated turmeric
½ teaspoon fresh grated ginger
3 Thai lime leaves
½ teaspoon sea salt

In a medium saucepan over high heat, put in all ingredients and bring to a boil. Reduce heat, cover, and simmer for 30 minutes. Remove from heat and let stand for 10 minutes. Discard the lime leaves, fluff with a fork, and serve.

Taste-Bud Tantalizers

Salty, sweet, bitter, sour, umami—the notes that keep your taste buds singing. Slowing down to savor allows you to really discover the levels of flavor that are inside of every bite. Chewing your food thoroughly and moving it around inside your mouth brings the taste buds to life and unlocks the essence of your food. If you're too hasty to get the next bite in, you're liable to miss how deeply satisfying each bite can be.

Festive Fruit Salad with Fresh Herbs

Rarely do we think of combining herbs with fruit, but this is a whole new way to wake up your taste buds and highlight some of the flavors of the fruit you never even knew existed. This simple combination is not only a palate pleaser, but it engages many of your other senses—it's a beautiful color combination that will delight your eyes, you'll pick up aromas that are fresh and sweet, and you can certainly pick at it with your hands. String the fruit onto skewers and sprinkle with herbs for a more tactile experience.

 Pairing herbs with fruit is easy and fun, so don't be afraid to experiment. Here are a few helpful hints for winning combos:

- Basil: vibrant flavor that goes well with kiwi, strawberries, and peaches

- Mint: complements most fruits and goes particularly well with berries and melons

- Cilantro: a more daring choice, but great with mangoes and other tropical fruits like pineapple and papaya

MAKES 6 SERVINGS

1 ripe cantaloupe, seeded, cut from the rind, and cut into 1-inch cubes
2 cups fresh blueberries

2 cups kiwifruit (green or golden, or both!), peeled and cut into rounds
¼ cup fresh chopped basil
2 tablespoons fresh chopped mint

Combine all fruit in a large bowl. Add the basil and mint and gently toss.

Divide into six bowls and serve.

Portobello-Wrapped Dates

Thank goodness this appetizer is so rich because otherwise it would be impossible to stop eating it. This is the ideal sweet-savory-salty combo. It hits every note perfectly and the flavor balance that comes from the extreme sweetness of the dates, the umami of the mushrooms, and the subtle saltiness of the nut cheese is exquisite. It's a vegan play off bacon-wrapped dates with goat cheese, and even bacon lovers (I guess that's almost everyone) won't feel like there's anything missing.

MAKES 12 SERVINGS (2 DATES PER SERVING)

2 large portobello mushrooms

2 tablespoons olive oil (or use olive oil spray)

¼ teaspoon sea salt

24 Medjool dates

4 ounces herbed nut cheese (I'm a fan of NuCulture or Treeline, but there are lots of good options)

Preheat the oven to 350 degrees F.

Slice the mushrooms into thin strips (about ⅛ inch thick). Spread the strips on a baking sheet. Baste or spray with the oil. Flip the strips and baste or spray the other side. Sprinkle with the salt and bake for 5 minutes.

Carefully remove the pits from the dates and scoop nut cheese into the centers of the dates. Remove the mushrooms from the oven and wrap each date in 2 strips of the mushroom, so each date is completely covered. Place them back on the baking sheet and return to the oven for 10 minutes. Remove and serve warm.

> *PRO TIP: If you really do wish to emulate the bacon-y flavor, use a smokier nut cheese. NuCulture actually makes a Bacony Chipotle Creamy Cashew Spread (sans the bacon). Make sure you use the spreadable nut cheese, not the grated vegan cheese substitutes.*

Citrus-Fueled Rocket Salad

As the name implies, this is not your average salad. "Rocket" is the more descriptive name the Brits use for arugula, which has a peppery kick that is best tempered with a bit of sweetness (featured here in the honey and grapefruit) and a little bit of tangy brightness (enter the Meyer lemon). If you've never had kohlrabi, it has a mild cauliflower-like flavor and the texture is much like a turnip. In fact, you could replace them with baby turnips when in season (and even toss the turnip greens in with the arugula).

MAKES 4 SERVINGS

For the dressing
¼ cup extra-virgin olive oil
2 teaspoons stone-ground mustard
Zest and juice (from 1 Meyer lemon)
1 teaspoon honey
¼ teaspoon sea salt
¼ teaspoon freshly ground black pepper

For the salad
6 cups loosely packed arugula
1 medium kohlrabi, peeled
1 large avocado, pitted and cut into cubes
1 ruby red grapefruit

To make the dressing, in a small bowl, whisk together the oil, mustard, lemon juice, zest, honey, salt, and pepper.

Put the arugula in a large bowl. Spiralize or shred the kohlrabi and toss in with the greens. Drizzle the dressing over the greens and toss until well coated. Gently mix in the cubed avocado. Divide the salad onto four plates.

Using a serrated knife, cut the peel away from the grapefruit, removing the thick white membrane. Carefully cut the membrane away from each grapefruit segment. Divide the grapefruit segments and arrange on the four salad plates.

> PRO TIP: This citrusy dressing is very versatile and can be used with any combo of mixed greens, or to drizzle over one of your Beauty Bowls (page 112). Make extra and store it in fridge for up to 2 weeks.

Garnet Yam Stacks with Kimchi Peanut Sauce

I know what you're thinking. *Kimchi peanut sauce?! Are you kidding?* That's what I thought, too, when I first heard about this idea from Firefly Kitchens' kraut creators. Actually, I came about it indirectly from a client who had been trying to fall in love with fermented foods for a long time. She took a cooking class, tried some version of the peanut sauce, and became a believer. I fully embrace the notion of creating unexpected flavor combinations using fermented foods, so this is right up my alley. I'm wimpy when it comes to spiciness, but the peanut butter tempers the kimchi. Broccolini has an inherent bitter note to it (as do all cruciferous veggies), but that gets outplayed by the sauce that the earthy sweet yam is resting upon.

MAKES 6 SERVINGS

1 large garnet yam

1 tablespoon plus 2 teaspoons
  avocado oil

2 bunches broccolini, finely chopped

½ teaspoon sea salt

For the kimchi peanut sauce

1 cup kimchi

½ cup unsalted peanut butter
  (creamy or crunchy)

2 teaspoons tamari

½ cup vegetable broth

½ cup water

Preheat the oven to 375 degrees F.

Slice the yam into rounds (about ½ inch thick) and spread on a baking sheet. Baste the rounds with 1 tablespoon of the avocado oil until well coated on both sides. Bake for 15 minutes, then broil on high for about 5 minutes, flip the rounds, and broil the other side for another 5 minutes, until they begin to brown and crisp. Remove from oven and set aside.

(CONTINUED)

(CONTINUED)

To make the kimchi peanut sauce, in a food processor or blender, combine the kimchi, peanut butter, tamari, and vegetable broth. Blend until smooth, adding the water to thin as necessary.

In a medium sauté pan over medium-high heat, heat 2 teaspoons of avocado oil. Add the broccolini and salt and sauté until broccolini is tender, about 5 minutes.

Portion out a generous spoonful of broccoli onto each yam round. Drizzle the peanut sauce over the top and serve.

PRO TIP: If you prefer a spicier peanut sauce, use stronger kimchi and/or add red pepper flakes when you are blending the peanut sauce.

Golden Beet Ribbons with Sun-Dried Tomato and Basil

I recently burned out on zucchini noodles. I got a little overzealous with my spiralizer and I made one too many zoodle dishes. Not quite ready to hang up my spiralizer, I discovered that golden beets are the perfect texture to stand in as an al dente pasta substitute. I don't have anything against pasta; I just like to find clever ways to make veggies the main event in any dish. This recipe does call for roasted garlic, which takes 45 to 50 minutes, so be sure to give that a head start. There's a beautiful sweetness to this dish from the beets, roasted garlic, and peas. The sun-dried tomatoes provide the acid to complement the sweet, oregano lends a pungent, earthy kick, and the basil brightens the whole thing up.

MAKES 4 SERVINGS

1 head garlic
1 teaspoon extra-virgin olive oil
1 ounce dried mixed mushrooms
3 medium golden beets
½ cup sundried tomatoes packed in
   olive oil
1 cup frozen petite peas

1 cup packed fresh basil leaves
2 teaspoons fresh oregano
1 teaspoon sea salt
½ teaspoon freshly ground black pepper

Special equipment
Spiralizer

Preheat the oven to 375 degrees F.

Slice the top off the head of garlic to expose the cloves. Drizzle with oil and wrap the head in aluminum foil. Place in the oven and roast for 45 to 50 minutes.

Put the mushrooms in a small bowl and add 1½ cups hot water. Allow to sit for 45 minutes, while the garlic is roasting. Add water to the mushrooms as needed if you find that it absorbs before the garlic is roasted. The goal is to rehydrate the mushrooms, so they shouldn't be dry or tough. Take a nibble and check out the texture.

(CONTINUED)

(CONTINUED)

Meanwhile, remove the stems and leaves from the beets and set aside. Spiralize the beets. Strip the stems from the leaves, roll the leaves, and chop into strips.

Measure out 2 teaspoons of the oil from the sun-dried tomatoes and drizzle into a large skillet over medium heat. Add the spiralized beets and sauté for 5 minutes, stirring frequently. Add the peas and rehydrated mushrooms, along with a couple tablespoons of the soaking water. Cover the skillet and allow to steam for 3 to 4 minutes, until the beets are tender.

Remove the garlic from the oven and squeeze 3 to 4 cloves onto a cutting board. Place the sun-dried tomatoes on the garlic and rough chop until the tomatoes and garlic are sufficiently smashed together. Transfer to the skillet, add the basil and oregano, and toss until the well coated. Season with the salt and pepper.

The
Sweet Spot

Nature provides so much natural sweetness for us to enjoy. Colonies of bees are hard at work, constructing hives that are dripping with honey. Maple trees spring syrup from a tap. And fruit, glorious fruit! A palate that's cleansed from processed foods and refined sugar can truly appreciate the pure sweetness of a perfectly ripe peach, a strawberry straight from the vine, or a handful of plump blueberries. Look beyond food to make sure there is an abundance of sweetness in your life.

Peachy Berry Hand Pies

Hand pies are great fun because it feels like you're getting your own little customized dessert, and it's just enough to make you happy without putting you over the edge. The gluten-free crust can be somewhat crumbly, so you may end up with rather rustic-looking hand pies, but that's part of the charm. You can also serve these with some Coconut Bliss ice cream or coconut whipped topping if you feel the need to cover up crumbly crusts or oozing filling. The most important part is that this combo is the perfect end note to any meal and is sure to hit the sweet spot!

MAKES 6 SERVINGS

1 large peach, peeled, pitted, and thinly sliced

¾ cup fresh raspberries

¾ cup fresh blackberries

3 tablespoons packed coconut palm sugar

1 tablespoon arrowroot powder

1½ cups gluten-free all-purpose flour, plus more for dusting

¼ teaspoon sea salt

½ cup plus 3 tablespoons coconut oil

3 tablespoons pure maple syrup

1 to 2 tablespoons cold water

Preheat the oven to 450 degrees F.

In a medium bowl, combine the peach, raspberries, blackberries, coconut palm sugar, and arrowroot and set aside.

In a small bowl, combine the flour and salt. In a large bowl, use either a hand mixer or a stand mixer fitted with the paddle attachment to beat the coconut oil until softened, about 1 minute. With the mixer on low speed, slowly add the flour mixture until incorporated. Add the maple syrup and cold water and continue beating until a soft dough has formed. (Alternatively, you can mix the dough by hand, kneading the ingredients to incorporate.)

(CONTINUED)

(CONTINUED)

Cover a baking sheet with parchment paper or lightly grease. Dust the parchment paper (or greased baking sheet) and your hands with flour. Divide the dough into six equal balls. Flatten one ball onto the top corner of the parchment paper or baking sheet and sprinkle with more flour. Roll the dough into a disc that's about ⅛ inch thick and 4 to 5 inches in diameter. Spread 2 large spoonfuls of the fruit mixture into the center, leaving ½ inch of dough around the edges. Fold the dough over to enclose the filling. Press the dough tightly closed with your fingers, then crimp the edges all the way around with a fork to seal. Repeat with the remaining dough balls and fruit, spacing them evenly on the parchment-covered baking sheet. In the top of each pie, cut a small vent (about four ½-inch cuts in a row).

Transfer the baking sheet to the oven and bake for 20 to 25 minutes, until the crusts are golden brown and the filling is bubbling from the vents. Cool before serving.

Tropical Smoothie Bowl with Toasted Coconut

Do you like piña coladas? Well then, you're gonna love this bowl. It's seemingly sinful, tropical, and festive all at once, and it really *does* hit the sweet spot. You could certainly have this for breakfast, but I like to stick with a savory breakfast and use the tropical smoothie bowl as a dessert. If your whole family is sitting around eating ice cream, you can just emerge from the kitchen with the bowl that looks like it came straight from paradise. You can even put a tiny umbrella in it for maximum envy.

MAKES 2 SERVINGS

½ cup coconut flakes, divided

1 frozen banana

½ cup frozen pineapple

½ cup frozen mango

½ cup frozen strawberries

1 to 1½ cups water

1 cup plain, unsweetened yogurt (can use dairy-free options like coconut, cashew, or soy)

1 cup granola

In a small, dry skillet over medium heat, put in ¼ cup of the coconut flakes. Stir frequently until the coconut flakes begin to turn light brown. Remove from heat and set aside.

Combine the banana, pineapple, mango, and strawberries in a high-powered blender and slowly add water until the mixture is well blended and the consistency of sorbet. Divide the blended fruit into two bowls. Top each bowl with ½ cup yogurt, ½ cup granola, and ¼ cup of the coconut flakes.

Cashew Cookie Bars

Dates and cashews are a match made in heaven, and when you top them with chocolate . . . forget about it! This is such a simple dessert that does not require any baking, but is every bit as satisfying as any cookies or cupcakes you'll ever eat. In fact, they're so sweet that I added some dried cherries to invite a hint of tartness to cut the sweet. The other brilliant thing about these cookie bars is that they're really, really *rich*, so you can be satisfied by mindfully eating just one.

MAKES 8 SERVINGS

2 cups raw cashews

2 teaspoons ground cinnamon

⅛ teaspoon sea salt

8 Medjool dates, pitted

3 tablespoons dried cherries

1 teaspoon coconut oil

1 (3.5-ounce) bar of dark chocolate
(73 percent cacao or higher)

Put the cashews, cinnamon, and salt into a food processor. Process until the nuts are finely ground, about 1 minute. Add the dates and process again until well combined; the mixture should have a thick, sticky consistency. Pulse in the dried cherries. Check to see if you can form a ball by rolling some of the mixture in your hands. If it falls apart easily, add more dates.

Grease an 8-inch square baking dish with the coconut oil. Transfer the mixture into the baking dish and gently press it into place. Melt the chocolate in a ramekin in the microwave or use a double boiler on the stovetop over low heat. Drizzle it over the cashew mixture. Spread evenly with a spatula, covering the entire cookie mixture.

Refrigerate for at least 1 hour and then cut into 3-by-1-inch bars. Keep leftovers refrigerated. They'll stay good in the refrigerator for about a week.

Discreet Beet Brownies

I first presented these red-velvet-looking brownies to a group of highly suspicious tasters in a cooking class I was teaching at a local co-op market. Many of them let me know in advance that they did *not* like beets, and I shouldn't be offended if they didn't eat dessert. I have to admit I was a bit nervous. It was fun to watch them take their first bites. Then second, then third. Not a crumb was left behind! Despite being best known for tasting "of the earth," beets really do add sweetness, so they're a better candidate for dessert than one might think. Let's face it, everything goes with chocolate, so it shouldn't be super shocking. The cinnamon is a nice surprise to the palate, and cardamom comes in as the finishing note.

If you feel like you're possessed by sugar, this is an excellent time to do the mindful eating activity on page 79. You can practice savoring a sweet dessert, truly appreciating the complex flavors, relishing every luscious bite, and not feeling like you need to eat the whole pan.

MAKES 12 SERVINGS

2 teaspoons coconut oil

1 cup water

3 medium crimson beets, scrubbed and trimmed (no need to peel)

1 cup gluten-free, all-purpose baking mix (e.g. Bob's Red Mill Gluten-Free Biscuit and Baking Mix)

½ cup cocoa powder

1 teaspoon baking powder

½ teaspoon baking soda

¼ teaspoon sea salt

1 teaspoon ground cinnamon

1 teaspoon ground cardamom

2 vanilla beans

1 cup grade B maple syrup

Preheat the oven to 350 degrees F. Use the coconut oil to grease a 9-by-9-inch baking dish.

Put the water in a pressure cooker and position the steaming rack. Quarter the beets and place them on the steaming rack. Cook on high pressure for 13 to 15 minutes. Release the steam and transfer the beets to a food processor or blender. Blend into a thick puree.

In a large mixing bowl, combine the baking mix, cocoa powder, baking powder, baking soda, salt, cinnamon, and cardamom. Slice open the vanilla beans and scrape the contents into the bowl. Add the beet puree and maple syrup and blend with a hand mixer until well combined.

Transfer the mixture into the baking dish and bake for 25 minutes, or until a toothpick comes out clean.

> PRO TIP: If you don't have a pressure cooker, you can use a steaming basket in a saucepan. Bring the water to a boil, place the beets in the steaming basket, and put a tight-fitting lid on the saucepan. Steam over medium heat for 20 to 25 minutes, until beets are easily pierced by a fork.

Chocolate Hazelnut Pops

Hazelnuts are my absolute favorite nuts to mix with chocolate. Ferrero Rocher and Nutella really got it right. These homemade pops are fun to eat and can satisfy a sweet tooth in the blink of an eye. Roasting the hazelnuts and removing the bitter skins elevates the natural sweetness and prepares them for the plunge into the bitter dark chocolate. You can play with adding other ingredients to the nut butter, like dehydrated strawberries or dried currants or cranberries.

MAKES 8 SERVINGS

2 cups raw hazelnuts (look for the round hazelnuts, not oblong)
¾ cup dark chocolate chips

Special equipment
8 short skewers or popsicle sticks
Double boiler

Preheat the oven to 350 degrees F.

Spread the hazelnuts on a baking sheet and roast for 10 minutes, until they just begin to brown. Transfer the nuts to a clean dish while they're still warm. Wrap the pile of nuts in a towel and aggressively massage them to remove the bitter skins. Transfer to a food processor or blender and blend to the texture of almond butter.

Roll the mixture into 1-inch balls and place each individual ball on a short skewer.

Melt the chocolate using a double boiler (or microwave). Dip the hazelnut lollipops in the chocolate so that they're well coated and lay them out on a sheet of wax paper to cool and solidify. You can transfer to the refrigerator or freezer. These will keep for 5 days in the refrigerator or 4 weeks in the freezer.

Adventurous Eating Awaits You

Hopefully some of the recipes in this book introduced you to some exciting and novel foods that will now become part of your regular repertoire. It's true that variety is the spice of life and we're fortunate enough to have an almost endless bounty of tasty, tantalizing foods to sample. Think of yourself as an anthropologist in the garden, a pioneer in the kitchen, and a gastronomer at the table. Trying new things reminds you to engage your senses and invite mindfulness into every experience you have with food.

FOOD AS ART
Romanesco
Fiddlehead ferns
Chioggia beets
Watermelon radishes
Brussels sprouts on the stalk

HANDS-ON FOODS
Artichokes
Pomegranate
Jackfruit
Sushi
Ethiopian flatbread (injera)
Collard wraps
Stuffed endive

POP, SIZZLE, CRUNCH
Pickles (real fermented cucumbers)
Jicama
Kohlrabi
Pan-fried tofu
Crispy chickpeas
Kale chips
Macadamia nuts
Marcona almonds

AROMATIC PLEASURES
Fresh herbs (basil, rosemary, sage, mint, lemon verbena)
Fresh ginger
Roasted garlic
Thai lime leaves
Lemongrass

TASTE-BUD TANTALIZERS
Dried porcini mushrooms
Delicata squash
Meyer lemon
Seaweed (dulse, nori, wakame, hijiki)
Kimchi
Truffle salt
Nut cheese

THE SWEET SPOT
Figs
Dragon fruit
Dates
Persimmons
Mangosteen
Lychee
Manuka honey
Pure maple syrup

Acknowledgments

The entire time I was writing this book, I lovingly referred to it as my passion project. I became so convinced that mindful eating is the missing link to having a joyful and peaceful relationship with food that I couldn't wait to spread the word. In 2016, I pitched the concept and submitted my proposal to Gary Luke, who was the publisher of Sasquatch Books at the time (and has since retired). Gary's twenty-five-plus years of editorial experience was invaluable as he guided me through the process of creating my anti-inflammatory cookbooks. When he reviewed my proposal for *Mastering Mindful Eating*, he had questions—*a lot* of questions.

In fact, we discussed this book off and on for nearly two years, and with each thoughtful response to his questions the content for the book became stronger and stronger. Finally, he agreed to attend one of my mindful eating classes with Jennifer Worick, and that was where we sealed the deal. As fate would have it, as Sasquatch's new editorial director, Jen enthusiastically took on this project. Her guidance, encouragement, and humor took away any angst I had while writing this book.

I owe a debt of gratitude to all of my patients who have bared their souls and allowed themselves to be vulnerable enough to really explore their thoughts, feelings, and beliefs about food and eating. I am the student of my craft every time I sit across from a patient or facilitate a group discussion about mindful eating and I'm so appreciative that I get to be the conduit for this important information.

None of this would be possible if I didn't have such an incredible network of family and friends who provide unwavering support in everything I do. Most notably, my mom, who always has my back and reminds me every day that I'm doing exactly what I was meant to do, and my stepdad, who manages my mom's neuroses when she's worrying that I'm working too hard (or any of the many things she worries about). Elaine Mowery, who has offered more words of encouragement and praise than I'll ever deserve and made me believe that I could overcome any obstacle that stood in my way.

And finally, my amazing recipe testers who commit to the task and give incredible feedback: Amy Ecklund and Heather Harman, Esther Garcia Cuellar, Lisa Miller, Jeff and Sheryl Smith, the Avina family, Sandy Simpson, Rob and Julie Sweet, and Fawn Coussens, who provided me with sustenance when I was too busy writing to feed myself.

Resources

BODY POSITIVE RESOURCES

Body Image Movement. BodyImageMovement.com. Founded by Taryn Brumfitt, the Body Image Movement aims to end the global body-hating epidemic by inspiring people to embrace their bodies through documentaries, books, online programs, and educational resources.

Health at Every Size. HAESCommunity.com. A site with various resources and a pledge to advance social justice and create an inclusive and respectful community.

Strong Inside Out. StrongInsideOut.com. An online community to draw strength from, be a source of energy to encourage you, and provide momentum to support you on your journey through health.

The Body Positive. TheBodyPositive.org. Women on a mission to create a lively, healing community that offers freedom from suffocating societal messages that keep people in a perpetual struggle with their bodies.

MINDFUL EATING SUPPORT

Headspace. Headspace.com. An app that promotes mindfulness and has specific mindful eating activities to help you practice being present while eating.

The Center for Mindful Eating. TheCenterforMindfulEating.org. A nonprofit on a mission to help people achieve a balanced, respectful, healthy, and joyful relationship with food and eating.

CRAVINGS AND FOOD ADDICTIONS

Emotional Freedom Technique (EFT). Also known as tapping, this simple and effective technique uses acupressure on specific energy meridians on your body to signal your brain to calm down and let go of obsessive thoughts. Here are a couple of my favorite resources:

- Bernstein, Gabby. 2014. "How to End Sugar Cravings with EFT." *GabbyBernstein.com* (blog). February 2, 2014.

- *The Chalkboard.* 2018. "EFT Tapping for Cravings: A Simple + Effective Practice to Try on Yourself." November 27, 2018. TheChalkboardMag.com.

Hypnotherapy and Neuro-Linguistic Programming (NLP). These techniques can be extremely helpful for cravings and releasing unwanted beliefs or obsessive thoughts about food. Look for board certified clinical hypnotherapists through the National Guild of Hypnotists (NGH.net). Two that I refer to in the Seattle area are IntegrityCoachingandTraining.com and TempleHypnosis.com.

Bibliography

Alcock J., C. C. Maley, and C. A. Aktipis. "Is Eating Behavior Manipulated by the Gastrointestinal Microbiota? Evolutionary Pressures and Potential Mechanisms." *Bioessays* 36, no. 10 (October 2014): 940–49.

Arnsten A. F. "Stress Signaling Pathways That Impair Prefrontal Cortex Structure and Function." *Nature Reviews Neuroscience* 10, no. 6 (June 2009): 410–22.

Artiles R. F., K. Staub, L. Aldakak, P. Eppenberger, F. Rühli, and N. Bender. "Mindful Eating and Common Diet Programs Lower Body Weight Similarly: Systematic Review and Meta-analysis." *Obesity Reviews* 20, no. 11 (November 2019).

Bacon L., and L. Aphramor. "Weight Science: Evaluating the Evidence for a Paradigm Shift." *Nutrition Journal* 10, no. 9 (January 2011) [published correction appears in *Nutrition Journal* 10, no. 69 (2011)].

Brewer J. A., A. Ruf, A. L. Beccia, G. I. Essien, L. M. Finn, R. van Lutterveld, and A. E. Mason. "Can Mindfulness Address Maladaptive Eating Behaviors? Why Traditional Diet Plans Fail and How New Mechanistic Insights May Lead to Novel Interventions." *Frontiers in Psychology* 9, no. 1418 (September 2018).

Camilleri G. M., C. Méjean, F. Bellisle, V. A. Andreeva, E. Kesse-Guyot, S. Hercberg, and S. Péneau. "Intuitive Eating Dimensions Were Differently Associated with Food Intake in the General Population–Based NutriNet-Santé Study." *The Journal of Nutrition* 147, no. 1 (January 2017): 61–69.

Christel D. A., and S. C. Dunn. "Average American Women's Clothing Size: Comparing National Health and Nutritional Examination Surveys (1988–2010) to ASTM International Misses & Women's Plus Size clothing." *International Journal of Fashion Design, Technology and Education* 10, no. 2 (2017): 129–36.

Cotter E. W., and N. R. Kelly. "Stress-Related Eating, Mindfulness, and Obesity." *Health Psychology* 37, no. 6 (2018): 516–25.

De Filippo C., D. Cavalieri, M. Di Paola, M. Ramazzotti, J. B. Poullet, S. Massart, S. Collini, G. Pieraccini, and P. Lionetti. "Impact of Diet in Shaping Gut Microbiota Revealed by a Comparative Study in Children from Europe and Rural Africa." *Proceedings of the National Academy of Sciences of the United States of America* 107, no. 33 (August 2010): 14691–96.

Gabel K., K. K. Hoddy, N. Haggerty, J. Song, C. M. Kroeger, J. F. Trepanowski, S. Panda, and K. A. Varady. "Effects of 8-Hour Time Restricted Feeding on Body Weight and Metabolic Disease Risk Factors in Obese Adults: A Pilot Study." *The Journal of Nutrition, Health and Aging* 4, no. 4 (June 2018): 345–53.

Guo F., and W. T. Garvey. "Cardiometabolic Disease Risk in Metabolically Healthy and Unhealthy Obesity: Stability of Metabolic Health Status in Adults." *Obesity (Silver Spring)* 24, no. 2 (February 2016): 516–25.

Hobbes M. "Everything You Know about Obesity Is Wrong." *Huffington Post*, September 19, 2019. https://highline.huffingtonpost.com/articles/en/everything-you-know-about-obesity-is-wrong.

Holland G., and M. Tiggemann. "A Systematic Review of the Impact of the Use of Social Networking Sites on Body Image and Disordered Eating Outcomes." *Body Image* 17 (June 2016): 100–110.

Institute of Medicine (US) Committee on Examination of Front-of-Package Nutrition Rating Systems and Symbols; Wartella E. A., A. H. Lichtenstein, and C. S. Boon, eds. *Front-of-Package Nutrition Rating Systems and Symbols: Phase I Report* (Washington, D.C.: The National Academies Press, 2010). Chap. 2, "History of Nutrition Labeling." Available from https://www.ncbi.nlm.nih.gov/books/NBK209859.

Krajmalnik-Brown R., Z. E. Ilhan, D. W. Kang, and J. K. DiBaise. "Effects of Gut Microbes on Nutrient Absorption and Energy Regulation." *Nutrition in Clinical Practice* 27, no. 2 (April 2012): 201–14.

McLean J. A., S. I. Barr, and J. C. Prior. "Cognitive Dietary Restraint Is Associated with Higher Urinary Cortisol Excretion in Healthy Premenopausal Women." *The American Journal of Clinical Nutrition*, 73, no. 1 (January 2001): 7–12.

Naleid A. M., J. W. Grimm, D. A. Kessler, A. J. Sipols, S. Aliakbari, J. L. Bennett, J. Wells, and D. P. Figlewicz. "Deconstructing the Vanilla Milkshake: The Dominant Effect of Sucrose on Self-Administration of Nutrient-Flavor Mixtures." *Appetite* 50, no. 1 (January 2008): 128–38.

Nelson J. B. "Mindful Eating: The Art of Presence While You Eat." *Diabetes Spectrum* 30, no. 3 (August 2017): 171–74.

Noreen E. E., M. J. Sass, M. L. Crowe, V. A. Pabon, J. Brandauer, and L. K. Averill. "Effects of Supplemental Fish Oil on Resting Metabolic Rate, Body Composition, and Salivary Cortisol in Healthy Adults." *Journal of the International Society of Sports Nutrition* 7, no. 31 (October 2010).

Russell W. R., S. W. Gratz, S. H. Duncan, G. Holtrop, J. Ince, L. Scobbie, G. Duncan, A. M. Johnstone, G. E. Lobley, R. J. Wallace, G. G. Duthie, and H. J. Flint. "High-Protein, Reduced-Carbohydrate Weight-Loss Diets Promote Metabolite Profiles Likely to Be Detrimental to Colonic Health." *The American Journal of Clinical Nutrition* 93, no. 5 (May 2011): 1062–72.

Schaefer J. T., and A. B. Magnuson. "A Review of Interventions That Promote Eating by Internal Cues." *Journal of the Academy of Nutrition and Dietetics* 114, no. 5 (May 2014): 734–60.

Schwarz N. A., B. R. Rigby, P. La Bounty, B. Shelmadine, and R. G. Bowden. "A Review of Weight Control Strategies and Their Effects on the Regulation of Hormonal Balance." *Journal of Nutrition and Metabolism* 2011, no. 237932 (2011).

Thaler A., M. N. Geuss, S. C. Mölbert, K. E. Giel, S. Streuber, J. Romero, M. J. Black, B. J. Mohler. "Body Size Estimation of Self and Others in Females Varying in BMI." *PLoS One* 13, no. 2 (February 2018): e0192152.

Tomiyama A. J., T. Mann, D. Vinas, J. M. Hunger, J. Dejager, and S. E. Taylor. "Low Calorie Dieting Increases Cortisol." *Psychosomatic Medicine* 72, no. 4 (May 2010): 357–64.

Tylka T. L., R. M. Calogero, and S. Daníelsdóttir. "Intuitive Eating Is Connected to Self-Reported Weight Stability in Community Women and Men." *Eating Disorders* (March 2019) doi: 10.1080/10640266.2019.1580126.

Varady K. A. "Intermittent versus Daily Calorie Restriction: Which Diet Regimen Is More Effective for Weight Loss?" *Obesity Reviews* 12 (July 2011): e593–e601.

Zabat M. A., W. H. Sano, J. I. Wurster, D. J. Cabral, and P. Belenky. "Microbial Community Analysis of Sauerkraut Fermentation Reveals a Stable and Rapidly Established Community." *Foods* 7, no. 5 (May 2018): 77.

Index

Nicole M. Ryan Photography

About the Author

MICHELLE BABB is a registered dietitian, functional medicine nutritionist, and food enthusiast. She has a private practice in West Seattle where she spends a great deal of time debunking common dieting myths. Michelle specializes in mind-body nutrition, digestive disorders, and inflammatory conditions, but her primary goal is to help people create a more productive partnership with their bodies and form a healthier relationship with food.

Through her training at the Center for Mind-Body Medicine, Michelle learned to encourage patients to trust in the inherent wisdom of their bodies and use that wisdom to guide their lifestyle choices. She earned a master's degree in nutrition from Bastyr University, where she came to understand the true meaning of *food as medicine*.

Michelle has been teaching cooking classes for over a decade and delights in featuring novel or misunderstood foods in her featured recipes. Michelle is the author of two other cookbooks, *Anti-Inflammatory Eating Made Easy* and *Anti-Inflammatory Eating for a Happy, Healthy Brain*, and she also coauthored a delightful little book called *The Imperfect Perfectionist: Seasonal Secrets for a Happy and Balanced Life*. Learn more about Michelle at EatPlayBe.com.